Shelter

For Sin,

Shelter

Sam Stonich

Sarah Stonich

BOREALIS BOOKS

Borealis Books is an imprint of the Minnesota Historical Society Press.
www.mhspress.org

©2011 by Sarah Stonich. All rights reserved. No part of this book
may be used or reproduced in any manner whatsoever without written
permission, except in the case of brief quotations embodied in critical
articles and reviews. For information, write to Borealis Books,
345 Kellogg Blvd. W., St. Paul, MN 55102-1906.

The Minnesota Historical Society Press is a member of the
Association of American University Presses.

Manufactured in the United States of America

10 9 8 7 6 5 4 3 2 1

♾ The paper used in this publication meets the minimum requirements
of the American National Standard for Information Sciences—Permanence
for Printed Library Materials, ANSI Z39.48–1984.

International Standard Book Number
ISBN: 978-0-87351-775-1 (cloth)
ISBN: 978-0-87351-800-0 (e-book)

Library of Congress Cataloging-in Publication Data
Stonich, Sarah, 1958–
Shelter/Sarah Stonich.
p. cm.
ISBN 978-0-87351-775-1 (cloth : alk. paper) —
ISBN 978-0-87351-800-0 (e-book)
1. Stonich, Sarah, 1958– 2. Stonich, Sarah, 1958– —Family.
3. Ely Region (Minn.)—Biography. 4. Ely Region (Minn.)—Social life
and customs. 5. Wilderness areas—Minnesota—Ely Region. 6. Country life—
Minnesota—Ely Region. 7. Log cabins—Minnesota—Ely Region.
8. Writers' retreats—Minnesota—Ely Region. 9. Single women—
Minnesota—Ely Region—Biography. 10. Women authors, American—
Biography. I. Title.
F614.E4S76 2011
977.6'77—dc22
2010042911

FOR DAD

Old fishermen never die, they only smell that way.
—Plaque on the cabin wall

Oma tupa, oma lupa. One's own cabin, one's own freedom.

—Finnish adage

Shelter

One

One midnight when I was about sixteen and watching the late movie with Dad, I started to nod off. He rocked my shoulder. "Listenup" he said, pointing to the screen. I propped up to peer past the bowl of old maids to see Mr. O'Hara, redder than usual, lecturing his daughter.

"Scarlett, do you mean to tell me that Tara—that *land*—doesn't mean anything to you? Why, land is the only thing in the world worth workin' for, worth fightin' for, worth *dying* for, because land is the only thing that lasts!"

I could guess where Dad was going with this. To him, land meant the butt end of the Canadian Shield, north of north in the border country where he was born in 1910 and raised with his nine brothers and sisters. To me it was a boring place at the end of a tedious drive that led to the ledgerock lakes and the house where our grandmother who could cook lived. Getting there meant hours of driving over flat, non-scenic highway, with the worst stretch cutting through a vast bog that evoked the word *gulag*.

Besides our small yard in town, Dad didn't actually own any land. The lakeside acres our cabin perched on were leased from the power company. The cabin was tiny, painted the color of a

3

BandAid, with damp floors and a scary propane smell, though the outhouse, Dad would boast, was a two-seater. Of course a working plantation like Tara has value, but the stony crust that passes for land in our wedge of Minnesota had never struck me as worth working for. But *dying* for? I returned his nudge with a kick and flipped my back to the screen. I couldn't have cared less about land, let alone a neurotic cocktease who dressed in curtains.

Dad died just a few years later. A dozen years after that, my son was born. Even when he was a toddler, it was obvious what genes had jumped a generation to splash in Sam's gene pool. He had my father's disposition and steady stare, and once again I found myself living with a short, territorial homebody with quick wit and hairy legs.

As can happen after a person has a child, one's take on the world expands to include the notion of a future beyond one's own. As I watched my son grow, Dad's long-ago nudge began to fester. I reconsidered Scarlett O'Hara, struck by that last scene when she has the revelation about place and permanence and independence that nearly transforms her from a Miss into a Ms. I didn't quite buy Scarlett's hammy swooning, but I was beginning to get the bit about land. My son missed out on having a grandfather, and he deserved to inherit something besides the gene for pattern baldness. What better legacy to unite one wispy-headed generation to another than land?

I began to revisit Dad's neck of the woods to search out some scrap to call our own, setting out with romantic visions and unrealistic expectations, meager funds and terrible timing. All I wanted was a sizable, private, pine-studded lot on a quiet lake, cheap, maybe with a funky old cabin on it, and I happened to want it just when land was fetching all-time high prices thanks to the demand of dot.comers with dot.incomes. I looked at dozens of properties in all ranges, from a hunting shack in the brush to an island lodge. Realtors put up with me. Two summers went by, then five. The hunt grew wearisome as prices peaked, or when we thought they'd peaked, since it was inconceivable that they could get any higher, yet they peaked and peaked again. I was edging toward a certain age and still didn't have a cabin when even my little sister did. I was the only one left knotty pining.

At home in St. Paul, Sam and I often made do by playing a game we called Cabin! Tucking in on cold nights, we'd tent under the covers, and off we'd go. It was always winter in Cabin! And we were usually lost and cold, tromping, sometimes limping through the woods in bad weather. We were often hungry since wolves always got the rabbit before we could and there were no convenience stores for miles. All was harsh and dark, but eventually, from a distance, tics of warm light from a vacant cabin would beckon through the trees to guide us, though we never questioned a warm beacon in a remote, off-the-grid wilderness. The cabin door was usually a bit of a challenge, and we sometimes had to break and enter, but we got in, got dry, and eventually got warm by rubbing sticks together to build a fire. There was nesting to do: wood to gather, beds to make. Miraculously there was always food, and if there wasn't water, we made it from snow. After fire-building and survival were out of the way, we'd settle in for the night, getting down to the business of doing exactly what we were doing when we commenced playing Cabin!, huddling under the covers with animal crackers, picture books, and juice boxes.

The closest I could come to giving Sam a real cabin experience was to take him to a rustic old resort not far from Ely, a string of small stone and log cottages with outhouses, cold-water kitchens, and a cement-block shower house near the lodge with flush toilets for the delicate. The cabins were a hundred years old, with bubbly window glass and checkered curtains. The squeaky floors had rodent holes, and porches doubled as bedrooms. It was inexpensive and entirely too inconvenient and folksy for the types we wanted to avoid: jet skiers, ATVers, and bass boaters. Visitors to Rustic Resort were a Birkenstocks-with-socks crowd of quiet librarians, musicians, and professors with old Volvos plastered with left-of-left bumper stickers. These guests were likely to be found reading, humming, birding along the paths, or draped on the rock ledge staring out at the lake, smelling vaguely like weed. Their teenagers babysat toddlers who careened diaperless in the sand, sticky with fruit leather and chocolate kefir.

One morning on the dock, Sam and I discovered a cocoon attached to a supporting beam. Whatever was inside was just beginning to wriggle its way out. We hung our heads over the end of the dock, rapt. For two hours we lay in wait, hoping for a butterfly but ready to settle for a moth. Eventually a bug-eyed, ugly worm emerged with two crusty black humps where wings should have been. Soon it started unrolling itself and pumping fluid from its body to the humps, which had softened to look more like scrunched-up hair. Like twin nets, the wings ever so slowly began to unfurl, each section filling with a clear sheen, erecting themselves into patterned scaffolds, the spaces within taking on the look of leaded glass as the fluid dried, hardening to opalescence. We'd been rewarded for our patience with a dragonfly!

Sam clapped. "Play it again!"

That cinched it. Sam understood operating systems and could program the VCR but knew nothing of weather or seasons, didn't know east from west, and surely had never sat through a sunset. He wasn't getting enough vitamin D. It was no longer just a desire—we *needed* a cabin.

We returned to Rustic Resort for a number of years. Our favorite cabin had once been a schoolhouse, actually one of the less charming buildings, but it reminded me of a cabin Dad took us to before we had our own, where he once dressed up like a deep-sea diver to tackle a hornets' nest and where my sister Valerie made herself cry after throwing her allowance into the fire rather than the chicken bones she'd meant to.

The cabin at Rustic Resort wasn't insulated, and late one June I arrived to find ice in the sink and had to get a fire going before I could take off my jacket—the indoor thermometer read 33 degrees. I'd brought a swimsuit but neglected to pack mittens, and I ended up wearing socks on my hands while attempting to type. I had often thought this was exactly the sort of cabin I would want, but after that weekend I revised my dream to include hot running water and a bathtub.

When Dad was young, his family of twelve somehow managed to own an island on Lake Vermilion while living on a tailor's income. It had a stand of tall pine and a sturdy little house pulled over the ice by oxen. After the Depression, it fell into tax forfeiture—tragic at the time, but doubly so was our discovery in the nineties that it could have been reclaimed for the small sum of delinquent taxes. Dad never quite recovered from once having had land and losing it. Maybe the notion of land and its permanence holds more appeal as I age—perhaps drawn closer to the soil since that's where I'm headed anyway.

I drove back roads with real estate agents so often I knew what they took in their coffee. We walked logging trails and looked at little plots with shore-hugging cabins and trailer homes with views. Nothing they showed me was quite right. Not private enough, not rocky enough, not piney enough. I imagined their eyes rolling when my voice spilled from their answering machines: "I'll be up this week!" My favorite agent was Bill, who seemed to know every property and the attributes of every acre in the northern half of the county. During our trips, he'd talk and I'd listen. He'd known my family a little, so it was like going for drives with a distant uncle. I learned something new from Bill each visit, such as the Finnish dimensions for a traditional sauna or that the nasty, biting black fly actually has a function besides driving us insane: to pollinate blueberries. On one of our last outings, we spotted a moose just off the narrow dirt road, its nose to the ground, chewing. As its head popped up at our approach, it thwacked its rack on a tree limb. "Moose," Bill informed me, "eat moss and have shitty eyesight."

We watched lakeshore prices reach the point where I had to throw in the towel and say good-bye to my dream. Simply, I didn't have the money. Bill, either feeling sorry for me or tired of hauling me around, scraped up one final option and told me about relatively cheap acreage that wasn't listed, mineral rights land being sold by a local mining company. The land was on a tiny lake near the town where my grandparents raised their ten children and lived out their long lives. The parcels were being sold in large chunks, and since it was more land than I wanted or could afford, I recruited my friends Terry and Susan, who'd also been looking for lake property. We figured there would be advantages to co-ownership, like splitting the cost of property taxes and road improvements, pitching in on projects. We'd been good neighbors in the past; we'd gladly do it again.

On a bitter February day, we drove four hours north and set out on foot over an unplowed road with a photocopied map. We searched for the little lake, close enough to Tower that Dad would have fished it as a boy. The man from the land office had instructed us to follow the road until the lake was visible and to watch for the low shore and the one tree among thousands that had a blue ring and a lot number spray-painted on it. Easier said.

After an hour of walking in single-digit temperatures on legs like pilings, we found the low spot. I took up my binoculars and squinted across the lake to a parcel of rock and pine and not much else. The blue-ringed tree marked a steep hill fronting a forty-some-acre parcel of boreal forest and scrub. Some of the land, according to the map, was under the frozen lake. Just offshore, as if it had tumbled there, was an almost-island with stunted trees, stitched to the land by an area of dry reeds frozen in the sort of sluice mosquitoes prize. This rocky, bleak familiarity was enough to stir the specter of my father, who perched on my shoulder, his hands forming a megaphone to whoop through my woolen earflap as if I were the deaf one, "Heads up, Sally!"

There was the land, exactly as I'd imagined—remote, piney, and on a lake too small for motorboats. It had no driveway, no well, no septic, no power, no *anything*—it was offered *as is*. Raw land. The cost of making it habitable or even accessible would pile on top of a price that was already more than I'd budgeted for. Somehow I hadn't thought of such details, of reality.

There wasn't even a navigable path to it. Even Cabin! had paths.

What had I been thinking? It was clearly too remote, too rugged, and given the climate would be isolated for most months of the year. My instinct was to flee, but as I looked across the ice, I felt gnomish bootheels digging into my clavicle. In the same tone he'd used when claiming that my teeth would eventually straighten themselves out or that in certain countries I might be considered pretty, my father's voice insisted, *It's perfect.*

I made myself look up the scraggly hill of pine once more and, in a voice not quite my own, muttered, "Sold."

Two

On a dare, bush pilot Mel Toumela once landed his float-plane blindfolded and hung over on a ninety-degree Sunday morning. After gliding to a stop ten feet from his water slip, he jumped out onto the float to accept the stakes: one bent Camel Straight and the last warm Bud from his best friend's cooler.

Mel passed on this anecdote as if to reassure me, despite my just telling him about my fear of small aircraft. Maybe he was kidding. As he boasted of more derring-do, I wondered when he'd start doing what pilots do pre-flight, like inspect the switches and buttons that run the engine, make sure there's enough fuel, or check that the bolts bolting the little aircraft together were really bolted.

But we took off with no such precautions, just groundless faith we would return. After all, Mel has flown since he was a teenager, first ferrying passengers to and from remote fishing camps, then, after actually getting his pilot's license, joining up with search-and-rescue missions. Later he trained to drop chemicals onto wildfires. Mel bought his first plane in his early twenties and now, in semi-retirement, says he only flies when he wants with what passengers he chooses. He nodded at me in such a way that I should be aware that a ride in his plane was the highest compliment he dished out.

Mel has strayed from the border lakes area only a few times, first to fly for an airline based in Minneapolis, a job he endured for either six months or six weeks—he claims he can't remember. He says he'd rather skim this northern swath every day than fly across the continent. This is a land he considers more or less *his*, proudly claiming to know the terrain better than he knows his own wife's backside.

The plan was to fly over the newly purchased acres on a lake too tiny for Mel to land on, just east and south of Lake Vermilion and twenty miles as the crow flies from Ontario. I also wanted to see the blowdown from the 1999 storm that took down whole forests within the park. As we rose far above Mel's lake, I began to take in the scope and mass of the forest below. Mel has real and historical ties to this land. I have familial ties but share none of his sense of ownership. He's lived here all his life and earned his wings around the time I was a toddler. As a child, I spent summers here, oblivious to anything beyond my sticky reach. My teenaged visits were spent belly-up on a swimming raft, sunglasses smudged with Coppertone and headphones thumping Fleetwood Mac or the Boss to drown out any natural sound. But on the day of my flight with Mel, I *needed* to become connected, suffering a case of buyer's remorse after signing a loan agreement for a tract of remote, roadless land when I'd only intended to buy a little cabin. The previous year had been intense and exhausting. I was facing a divorce and single parenthood, and somehow during all that, I decided to throw myself at a long-term project requiring more money than I had and perhaps more energy than I could spare. The land was going to be a labor of love, except suddenly I wasn't feeling the love. As we gained altitude, I needed every assurance I'd done the right thing, was landing in the right place.

As if reading my thoughts, Mel, a font of malapropisms, piped up, "You know that saying, you can't see the forest for the timber? It's the truest thing; you can't see a place proper 'til you're far enough away from it. And I don't mean just from a height." He shook his head. "After I saw what I did of the world, I realized it don't get any better than this right here." Mel winked. "Hell, I'd be happy to die in this plane right now with my cap on."

I inhaled most of the air in the small compartment. Surely he hadn't intended to use the words *die* and *plane* in the same sentence?

As we skirted the no-fly zone, I could make out the pattern of the terrain and the gouges left by great glaciers: clawed wounds that wept to their brims to form countless lakes and ponds; silky scars of creeks wedged diagonally between ledges of granite, pale tamarack bogs and pine. The Boundary Waters Canoe Area was so named in 1958, an improvement over its dull designation as a National Roadless Primitive Area. In 1978, the Wilderness Act established regulations much as they are today, making the Boundary Waters almost completely free of motorized boats, land vehicles, and man-made structures. The recent addition of a second *W* makes it BWCAW—*W* for "wilderness," in case it's not obvious. Most just call it "the Boundary Waters." From the vantage point of over a thousand feet, it comprises a piney, million-acre forest spreading in all directions, at one glance primeval, awe-inspiring, and a little terrifying. As we flew, I recalled another instance of awe from a great height. Years ago, on the windy observation deck of a Manhattan skyscraper I clung to the railing while being lashed by my own hair and took in the endless stain of urban America, the best and worst of civilization: man and machine, commerce and power, all churning in the grids of chockablock architecture on streets of unceasing movement. To a midwesterner, the density was choking. Noise pummeled from every direction, constant enough to seem part of the air. Suddenly I was merely a dot of humanity, just one of hundreds of thousands like those below in the streets, just another nano-particle with arms and legs suddenly needing to vomit.

Looking out from Mel's little plane, struggling to get my bearings in a corresponding remoteness, I questioned my significance again and once again came up short. I concentrated on the view: more water than land, lakes connected by rills and rivers, many originating in Minnesota but narrowing to a close in Ontario, glittering threads that baste the two countries together, American waters flowing north above the Laurentian Divide to feed over five hundred lakes of Quetico Provincial Park. The Boundary Waters has two thousand lakes, and Mel pointed to some, ticking off the names of a few, which left me puzzling over how they ended up being called Ash Dick, Swollen Ankle, Squirm, Calamity, or Meat. Earlier, Mel had tapped over a map, showing me Sarah Lake, crowing, "There, there's your own. If that one don't suit you, there's another somewhere west of here but without the *h*."

I imagine the thrill my father would have had to see this from the air. In the thirties, he'd canoed and portaged these lakes as a wilderness guide. While guiding is no easy job now with Kevlar canoes and freeze-dried meals, back then it had to have been a back-breaking hump. The canoes were wood and canvas and dreaded for their weight. Dad was five foot seven and a hundred fifty pounds soaking wet, yet he would have toted heavy canvas tents, food preserved in steel cans, and oak folding cots. He and his mates would have dragged it all overland on rough paths that make current-day portages seem like light rail. Somewhere in the family archives is a photo of him posing next to waist-high tonnage of camp gear, tan faced and bright eyed, with khakis tucked into knee-high, Mountie-style boots. He is smiling at something beyond the camera, looking happy, at home, and utterly exhausted.

Dad had flown during WWII as an officer in the army air force, a navigator on bombing missions with targets in the Asian Pacific. I know very little about his war years except that he was based in New Guinea, where his unit hired local aboriginals, paying them nickels a day to clean and cook and do their laundry, a brief stint of luxury Dad often fondly recalled when folding his boxers on our dining room table. He didn't talk about the war, and I don't think he ever flew again afterward; whether intentionally or not, I can't know. Looking down over the green wilds he once paddled, I imagined he might have made an exception to see his old stomping grounds from the air.

Mel banked the plane toward the area where the storm blew down old-growth pine over 140,000 acres. I took photographs as we skimmed islands and broad hillsides of flattened timber, tinder for potential firestorms. As far as we could squint, the landscape looked like sculpted shag strewn with toothpicks. For the first time during our flight, Mel had nothing to say. The devastation made me think of bombed cathedrals.

After we swept back over spared portions of forest, Mel's mood lightened, and he began rattling off regional lore in his singsong Minnesota accent, saying "yaaa" for yes and "dose" for those, dialog from *Fargo* at double speed. A favorite anecdote concerned the 1968 Olympic hockey team, comprised of Minnesota and Massachusetts boys who could barely understand one another for their conflicting accents. A few were confused enough to ask why, if this was the U.S. team, did they have teammates from foreign countries?

Then he told the story about the bear that broke into his house, ate a pack of cigarettes, and drank most of a twelve-pack of Pabst. When Mel's wife came home from book club, she heard snoring and Leno in the living room as usual and went to bed. After she and Mel were both roused by a clatter, they interrupted the bear just as he was finishing up a pound of ARCO coffee. Looking around at the mess, Mel's wife picked up the closest thing, a Dustbuster, and turned it on the bear, yelling, "I already have a husband!" The coffee and the fright were enough to loosen the bear's considerable bowels so that, as it fled, it left a wake of rank stew textured with undigested Parliament filters.

"Is that true?" I asked.

"Bears are afraid of Dustbusters? Goddamn right they are."

With exaggeration thick as pine pitch, Mel told more stories, and I skeptically jotted down his "facts." Later, when I double-checked, I found him fairly accurate, although the leading cause of death among the fur-trading voyageurs was *not* constipation, as he insisted.

Mel said something about swans, but my life vest had ridden up to dislodge my headset. I nodded, thinking he would show me some. He added something else, but each word was wrapped in static. Mel gave me a thumbs-up and we banked heavenward, a slow roller coaster climb, steep enough to press my belly button spineward. I idly examined the underside of a single low cloud, wondering if that was our destination, if the swans were above it, though surely we were too high for birds? Once I fumbled my headset back into place, I pressed my microphone button to ask, but the plane suddenly roared. We swooped in a sudden but graceful arc. The sky disappeared as we tipped below the horizon, and I was jolted forward, my armpits creased by harness straps. Mel didn't mean swans; he meant *swan dive*, though our trajectory wasn't very swanlike, more like a hawk aiming for the world's last mouse. I clamped my mouth and squinted, trying to keep my eyes and Cheerios in place. As we sped toward jagged rock and pine, I understood that the little plane would barely make a pinprick on the earth after the crash, barely a ripple should we hit water. The earth heals quickly here; brush grows over charred soil, swamps suck debris deep, dark waters draw wet curtains over whatever fuselages sink.

Our remains might never be found. I looked to Mel, who would share my fate as fish food or spruce mulch, but he only grinned. I reminded myself he was very much in control of his plane, a man who, while a risk taker of his own boasting, would never, ever endanger a passenger, though he might set out to scare the crap out of one.

I tried to cross my arms over the bulk of my vest, suspecting I wasn't the first passenger to be hazed in such a manner. Alert with adrenaline, everything was sharp-edged and clear. Not all that far below, I thought I could make out a loon's floating nest.

Gavia Immer, the common loon, Minnesota's mascot plastered on everything from mugs to garage door murals, embroidered on oven mitts, stuffed as plush toys, and printed on millions of lottery tickets like the one in my pocket, sure to be a winner once I'd splatted to my death. No one ever points out that the loon is possibly the most vicious state bird in the nation. It cannibalizes other waterfowl by spearing upward from the depths, its favored prey being a kabob of baby mallard. In spite of its maniacal laugh and *Redrum*-eyed, razor-beaked, devil-duck appearance, the loon is loved.

The plane lost altitude as if greased, falling toward a copse of spruce poised to perforate small aircraft. Just when I was able to make out cones among the boughs, the plane suddenly scooped up like a fishhook, like an amusement park ride, and once again we faced seamless blue sky.

The aerial map I'd been holding was a sweaty bouquet. I counted my breaths. Mel seemed a little disappointed I hadn't screamed or fainted, but it did take a moment before I could gather the spit to say, "Let's do it again!"

He sighed and soberly reminded me we'd been airborne for more than our allotted time and were now low on fuel.

"Low?" I asked.

Mel grinned. "Not *low*-low, just low."

With a wing-tip salute to all below, the plane veered south and away.

The finale of our flight was a swing over the land. The Lake looked like a miniature version of all the other lakes: another shiny claw mark, this one barely a scratch. From above, our acreage was a bumpy collection of poplar and pine. The small clearing near the shore could have been a rag dropped next to a puddle.

From the air it was nothing special. When Mel asked if I wanted to circle it again, I shook my head. We flew west over the big populated lakes, shorelines densely dotted with cabins, some modest, but an alarming number were log mansions with chemically treated lawns spilling down to water's edge. Over Vermilion we dipped to circle the island that belonged to my grandfather. The house was just visible through the trees. The island belongs to others now, though it still carries our family name.

Things here are slow to change.

We approached landing. Reflected sun under the wings made it seem we were held aloft by light. Nearing the dock where Mel won his famous bet, we disturbed a swimming beaver, hesitant to abandon the length of birch it was towing.

"Damn rodents." Mel leaned on a control that made the plane roar, scaring the beaver into diving under. He grinned and growled, "Take *that,* ya little bastard!"

Our flight was over.

Three

Sam was born in 1987, just as the Internet was launching, a digital-age baby who has never dialed a rotary telephone or tuned a radio with a knob. Arching a brow in my teenage son's direction, I realized that he likely could not climb a tree. He's tech-savvy and result driven, with good hand-eye coordination thanks to the Nintendo I was never, ever going to allow him to have. He squints when outdoors and sneezes through hay-fever season. My own childhood was spent seemingly doing nothing yet doing quite a lot, usually involving a mud puddle or a captive insect, inventing a hundred ways to beat boredom. At Sam's age, I was outside peeling birch bark to separate it into tissue-thin sheaves, or examining our dog's scalp to discover that the skin under the dark fur was dark, too, and wondering if I could get away with shaving it. I spent hours dismantling a fish spine or painting my hand with Elmer's and holding it sunward to dry, the reward being a molted skin of fingerprints and life-lines, a creepy glove to leave hanging on the neighboring cabin's doorknob.

I grew up in slow motion, with time to focus on small, inconsequential details and do small, inconsequential things: turn a rubber doll's head inside out to give it a haircut at the source, track the growth of a mold in a pine-paneled corner of the cabin, raid a gull's nest, intending to raise the chicks and train them as pets, only to find by the time I'd rowed back to shore that the eggs had smashed in the pocket of my windbreaker.

Sam's world was a far cry from mine and fanned open before him on the computer or wide-screen TV. Of course he needed more outdoor time to saunter or kick sticks; we all did. Did he know that just two hundred miles north lived actual bears and cougars? His knowledge of animals was limited to the Discovery Channel and our house pets: geriatric Bald Walter and Sam's own cat, Eyegore, often likened to a well-groomed stoner. Was it too late to make an outdoor kid of him, after twelve years spent mostly indoors? Probably. His gene pool was hardly aswim with athletes or outdoorsy types. His dad wasn't the ball-tossing, camping type. He was more likely to take Sam out for sushi or to a film fest than fishing or a baseball game. The closest Sam and his dad came to "sport" was stalking each other with increasingly larger Nerf guns—inside. We sent him to canoe camp and fly-fishing camp rather than teach him to paddle or cast ourselves. Withering to think now I was *that* sort of parent.

I secretly cheered Sam's sports apathy, grateful that I'd never be a hockey mom, that I'd have someone to hang out with at the library or coffee shop, that he would come of age with his own teeth.

As a mom, I hadn't listed fun and adventure high on my agenda. I'd only been hell-bent on Sam having what I hadn't had as a child: darling pajamas and stability. I mistook staying with his father for stability, right up until the day Sam asked, "Why be married if it isn't any fun?" It became apparent that holding the family together wasn't working. As parents, we were hardly setting any great example. From where Sam sat, marriage might be two people who reside in the same house when they are both in town, rarely fighting, rarely connecting, merely attempting to stuff the cracks where happiness might be.

After the divorce, the land took on more significance in our lives. I hoped Sam would at least *like* it, and though it was still just raw acreage, it was a tangible, certain something in uncertain times. It would become a haven, eventually a place Sam might bond to and maybe even take his own kids to one day. I had to remind myself that this land was an investment in his *future*, because at twelve, Sam wasn't eager to retreat to the woods where there were no comforts of home: no computer games, no toilet, not much of anything except a whole lot of nature.

When life has a tendency to crest high and crash down as it did through the first years of single motherhood, what helped more than the antidepressants and therapy was time spent here, where each stick of firewood burned took a little tension with it, each footfall on moss softened the worrisome edges. The yammering of birds drowned out abrasive thoughts. I became more absorbed by the place, saving me from becoming too self-absorbed. In small and not-so-small ways, the land allowed me to envision possibilities, independence, and maybe even happiness. The rhythm here, a metronome of natural sound, regulated me, kept the tempo of *normal* for me.

I reread the accounts of northern life that had influenced me as a girl, wanting to compare the observations in those books to see if their stories struck any new chords. Dad's old copies of Sigurd Olson and Helen Hoover books were long gone, so I tracked them down secondhand. I'd remembered reading Justine Kerfoot's quick little columns, which I was able to find conveniently bound into a single volume. I'd related to Helen Hoover's observatory style in *A Place in the Woods,* writing about the outdoors from inside, on the comfortable side of the window, which would be my preference. I could picture Helen's messy desk: coffee cup and ashtray and piles of books within reach, the author deep in thought until her husband came in to break the trance, bringing supplies and smelling of wood smoke and cold. I remember thinking that was the most romantic entrance ever. Reading Hoover's books as an adult, I caught more subtle underlayments. When the Hoovers had settled into their wilderness lives, Helen had been middle aged, like me. Childless, she eventually grew critter-happy, establishing a sort of soup kitchen for the wild, feeding every creature she could entice, not just with precious feed paid for with scant dollars and carried in to their remote site but as often with their own food. This maternal sacrifice for whatever baby-faced animals came romping to her door made me wonder if she wasn't a bit soft for the brutal realities of the north. I found I related better to her early books, when settling in and acclimating to the north was the challenge, when she seemed less barmy.

Justine Kerfoot seemed to me a fearless doer, a woman of more action than words. There are no frills to Kerfoot's writing, just portrayals of the nuts and bolts of wilderness life: her own adventures, those of others, and the amicable, necessary bonds between fellow northerners who are in it together. She wrote it more or less as it was, with few adjectives, but in a gossipy, friendly way, leaving the musing and poetry to others.

In the beginning of *The Voyageur's Highway*, Grace Lee Nute gifts the reader with a description of the north wearing some very nice outfits: "Her flowing garments are forever green, the rich velvet verdure of pine needles. In autumn she pricks out the green background with embroidery of gold here and scarlet there. Winter adds a regal touch, with gleaming diamonds in her hair and ermine billowing from her shoulders." Nute likens the north to a siren, suggesting that, sure, the place is beautiful, but it can be perilous, a poetic reminder to take care, and wear those life jackets lest the kayaks or canoes be dashed on the rocks.

Sigurd Olson's works seemed more purposeful and *male*, as if he needed to decode and translate the nature of nature in the way a man in love might try to figure out a woman. Reading his biography, I was not surprised to learn he had a dark side, that the wilderness was often a salve to the bruises of his depressive periods. I was surprised to learn how he'd struggled, and I felt a kinship, though his relationship to the land seemed a true and utterly serious one, as if he heard its very voice in his head, like some spruce whisperer.

In those first stages of ownership, I was turning to dead writers to try to make sense of where I fit in. Some days it felt like nostalgia had trumped sense to land me here. I had a deed bearing my signature on it and a debt in an amount I could have lived on for several years.

And while the hunt for land had been long, once I'd found myself half owner in a truly beautiful place, it all felt very sudden. For a while I merely *owned* it. Since I couldn't afford to build anything, it was mostly a place to visit and explore. I thought about camping, though my camping experience is nil and my outdoor skills are lacking, which seems to surprise many, the assumption being that growing up in northern Minnesota entails snowshoeing to school or skijoring through the bush to the trading post. I was never a girl scout, don't own a buck knife, and cannot fashion a tourniquet. What I'm really best at in the woods is *sitting*.

To build a serious campsite would have involved trekking in with axes, saws, shovels, and rakes to clear and level an area that would have required many, many buckets of gravel, also hauled overland. The place was mostly a day-trip site, a place to muck around and picnic on and explore when conditions were right. We'd bought the land having barely stepped a foot on it, only squinting northward from across the lake at the few piney acres fronting the shore, and those had been covered in snow at the time. The bulk of the land might have been wasteland as far as we knew, and indeed some of it proved nearly inaccessible, cut off by ridges, chasms, or bog. The more remote acres revealed their charms slowly as we were able to explore them.

The shoreline is the real draw. The little almost-island is a rather complete place on its own, like the Little Prince's asteroid. And just like his asteroid, the island is also the size of a house: a rough granite house about thirty feet across, a jam-packed hump that can take half a day to explore if you nose into the leprechaun ecosystem underfoot. One end of the island is domed and loaf-like, split in vertical fissures on one end, slices of rock fanning open like granite rye. The dark wedges of space between the stone are home to the island snake, beetles, worms, bugs with too many legs, and shudder-worthy blind albino whatnots.

Unprotected and windblown, many of the island trees are stunted or twisted, like the contortionist tree that twines down from its rock-bound roots before arching back upward again in tight elbow curves. Its needles are somewhat shorter than average, an adaptation to its nutrient-deprived roots and raw exposure, an example of evolution in action.

We swim and bathe off the east side of the island from a flat shelf of stone that drops off quite quickly. The underwater shelf is always slick with green fairy hair. Getting in is easy—just slip or jump. The coward's option is to scooch inch by inch down the slope until it drops off, when you sort of slide in like a Jello shot. Jumping or diving is preferable, the lungs seizing only for a moment, a longer moment in autumn or spring.

Getting out is another thing, mostly accomplished by belly-squirming back up over the slimy moss that's a veritable nursery for infant leeches—harmless, but leeches nonetheless. I bought a heavy, rubber-backed commercial rug like those found in building entrances and rigged it toboggan-fashion around the base of a tree so that, when rolled out over the stone and into the water, it offers some purchase and a leech-free exit. The rug rolls up neatly when not in use, tucked behind the tree it's tethered to.

For its size, the island has a surprising variety of North American trees, most standing in pairs, as if invited by Noah to a timber mixer: poplar, red pine, white pine, birch, balsam, black spruce, cedar, oak, Juneberry, and a single, tenacious little maple. This is not toothsome soil, yet somehow flora abounds. The dwarfed ferns root themselves into soil-free cracks to live on rainwater; the lichen and mosses survive on dew. Every living thing on the island seems to struggle in the climate and has grown slightly distorted from the constant tug of the two directions of scarce nutrients: sun and water.

The jewel of the island is easy to miss and small enough to step on: a natural, perfect, white pine bonsai, only six inches tall, though it's maybe ten, fifty, or a hundred years old. When the Japanese cultivate bonsai by root stunting, contortion, bondage, and routine amputation, they're simply replicating the environment of our island. Even the needles of the little pine are truncated to a third their normal length. This Gidget tree might be my favorite of all on the land, although I'm very fond of its towering uncle a quarter mile away, a hundred-plus-foot white pine that centers the lakeside acres.

Between the island and the shore is a swath of reeds and mud and water, its depth dependent on the lake level, which depends on how clogged the culvert at the west end of the lake is, which depends on how busy the beavers have been. You can walk between the island and shore in rubber boots, but there are a few surprise spots where you'd regret not having hip waders.

From the piney plateau above, the whole of the island isn't entirely visible through the foliage. Now and then I'll catch glimpses of the blue kayak or Sam sitting on the island with his feet in the water and a book in hand, moments surpassing my best, most hopeful visions for this place.

Paralleling our shoreline midway between building sites is another piney area, steep edged and tough to reach, cut off from approach by a cliff, which is too bad, for with its canopy pine, ledge rock, and view it would be an ideal building site. Below the site hammocks a valley of poplar and birch, a favorite of the beavers, with many chewed tree trunks strewn helter-skelter in their wakes.

Beaver are not beloved here, with most people considering them for what they are, America's largest rodent. Besides man, beavers are the only mammal able to significantly alter their environment and are just as careless and wasteful as we are. A single beaver can shear up to seventeen hundred trees a year—tens of thousands of board feet of lumber—consuming only the leaves and smallest twigs, abandoning the trunks to rot where they fall. Beavers also mess with lake levels. It's not exactly legal to eradicate beaver, making us yearn for the days of the fur trade, when trap-happy voyageurs could rid an entire lake of them *tout de suite.* According to the DNR, trapping fishers, pine marten, and fox all have seasons in Minnesota. You can kill a bobcat, even bag a badger if you can find one, as if there are extra. You can trap a beaver, but it is widely known that you cannot shoot a beaver, and it is widely ignored when they are shot. To the mirth of the local DNR staff, one of our more sympathetic neighbors (who will never live it down) called to inquire if there might be a beaver relocation project.

After the spring snowmelt and the winning date of the ice-out contest passed, we waited for the mud to crust over, finally able to tromp areas beyond the old logging road that cuts diagonally through our acres, roughly separating them into sections: the lake side, comprising about a fifth of the total land, and the back forty, lovely but rugged. Over the steep ridge from the beavered-out valley is a moody cedar bog, a place I find darkly handsome, not quite sinister, but mysterious like Colin Farrell or Don on *Mad Men*. The cedar bog was once home to the only human resident we know of. Bog Man lived here during the Elvis era by our best estimation, but by the time we arrived, his shack was long gone, his possessions hauled away or sunk under the cover of moss. Left behind were his bedsprings, scraps of metal, parts of an old stove, and more bottles than an off sale. Bog Man's choice of building site—dank, dark, and spongy—didn't make much sense until our resident geologist mentioned there was likely a spring nearby. And though we can't locate it, we know it's there, for even during the warmest, driest weeks of summer, the water between the cedar roots has movement and is clear and cool. We don't know who Bog Man was, or whether he'd owned the land or just squatted, whether his shack was a year-round home or just his seasonal *pied-à-terre.*

We were a family drawn to bogs. During Sam's phase of being obsessed with all things medieval, he inhabited an imaginary kingdom that included a bog called Fetid Stew. Sir Sam and the Knights of the Formica Table all had one enemy in common: problems of the sort only a six-year-old could think up. Someone in the kingdom had been bequeathed a wish, and since the recipient wasn't the sharpest arrow in the quiver, that *adult* had wished the river running through the Kingdom of Barns be *transformated* from water into chocolate malt! Great—until everyone had their fill, got tummy aches, and came down from their sugar highs only to realize that the fish would *snuffocate* because malt can't translate through gills, horses couldn't be watered, and crops couldn't be *irritated*. Sam, along with Sir Batty (stuffed bat and sleeping companion, tragically kidnapped during a car trip a few years later), was one of the bravest knights, unafraid of the dark.

Sam and Sir Batty put their noggins together and came up with a plan. They would divert the river into the bog! And so the bog became a repository for All Bad Things, where the evil troll lived, and since bog = stinky, wet, and yucky, it was where one was sent for punishment. Bandits who stole Princess Jennifer's wand were banished to Fetid Stew, a plague of rogue pterodactyls were captured and sunk in it, and so on. Bogs in general got an undeserved bad rap until we began visiting a nature preserve that had a real bog. The good bog had marsh birds with chopstick legs, bog rosemary, and spongy peat under an undulating shag of billiard green moss. There was a boardwalk on which to lay and watch the pitcher plants drink. We changed our tune then about the lowly bog, Sam admitting bravely, "I could do a time-out here."

And here we had our very own bog. Nothing as grand, but mossy just the same. The bog partially wraps the base of the cliff backing the plateau, where stones covered in nappy moss have tumbled down into the shade, making navigation a slippery endeavor, where hybrid rubber boots with golf cleats would be the ticket. From the bog, there are three directions to go: west, north, and south. South is a low spit of land and one of the few places on the lake where it's easy to land a canoe because the water is shallow with a gravelly bottom. The little promontory there has a fire pit, much used over the decades by trespassing beer lovers leaving all vintages of cans, many with old-country names like Schlitz, Blatz, and Pabst and one rusted, barely legible Old Bohemian.

These days the promontory has two melon-colored Adirondack chairs and a red canoe and could be a page from a tourism brochure. The path from the promontory leads to a steep hill of deciduous hardwoods, black spruce, and balsam. The path levels out at the hill's rocky apex, where Terry and Susan had chosen their building site, high above the westernmost shore. Facing straight east, they have the long view, making The Lake seem larger than it is.

Conditions aren't often ideal for exploring. Winter's not really an option since snow restricts any movement beyond the plowed logging road. While someone more adventuresome might strap on snowshoes, there are steep slopes and random blast holes left in the wake of early mining exploration, varying in size from trough to tanker, and often deep enough to break a leg should you fall in, or give you a good soaking since many fill with water after a hard rain. Having no idea how numerous or random the pits were, I played it safe in winter, sticking to the road and trails.

Early spring is too soggy for exploring, and late spring is too buggy. In summer, the thick brush turns any jaunt into a trail blazing, best embarked on with gloves, loppers, and plenty of DEET. Autumn is the best time, though in any season there's a good chance of getting lost. The iron content in the rocks is so high that compasses fail, only sometimes hinting at north in cattywampus stabs of the needle. So *sans* compass or GPS, I would venture out, noting where the sun was *when* there was sun. I soon discovered tree moss cannot be counted on to indicate north; those with any on their trunks wear it twirled in dervish skirts as if *every* direction might be north. When going very far, I don't go alone.

We owned the land for almost a year before discovering its best feature, one we didn't so much stumble onto as stumble *up*. Paralleling the logging road along our rear acreage is a high ridge of Precambrian rock well curtained by trees and obscured from the road below. Finding reasonable access to it is difficult. I've approached from several angles and found only one route that slopes rather than climbs, but I didn't have neon marking tape with me and haven't been able to locate the route since. The most direct and difficult way is straight up from the lowest point on the road via a very narrow path lined with aspens to hoist yourself along. The path ends at a short cliff the height of a bus, with a switchback zagging the rest of the way. Once on the zenith—usually with heart still a-thump—you'll see the climb was worth the effort. Spreading southward is a forest of ridges, with the Laurentian Divide just six miles away. On a clear day, you can see ten or fifteen miles. In summer, the view is an even-toned green canopy, but in autumn, drifts of tamarack make long mustard streaks and oaks pop like rust spots among the yellow aspen. Maples here turn not quite the usual red orange but a paler peach version, like a bare, bitten lip. The stands of pine are best delineated after their deciduous neighbors swap out their green for harvest moon colors. What you can see of The Lake beyond the poplar skirt belting the ridge looks narrow as a run of foil. Only after the aspen quake themselves naked is the full breadth of The Lake visible.

The ridge is shaped roughly like a parade of brontosauruses lumbering nose to tail through the canopy. It is perhaps a thousand feet long, running alongside a second, shorter ridge directly north, which I only know of for having been lost between the two, pinballing between them like a bug in a gutter until finally the sun broke out to show where west was.

It would be great to watch a storm from this height, and an idiot just might, but I have a healthy fear of lightning, and every pine on the ridge is a potential target. Weather travels straight west to east here, thumbing in on a stiff breeze that's brisk and consistent enough to make us dream of wind turbines. A turbine could provide enough electricity for us to fire up the holy grail of all appliances: a refrigerator. A gray-water pump system runs a close second on our wish list, usually while stumbling from the car with five-gallon jugs pulling our arms ape long. A pump would pull water up the hill for dishwashing and *showers.* It's hard to disguise envy when visiting the plumbed and electrified cabins of friends who are on the electrical grid, awed as they run taps and blithely flip switches to power up such trifles as toasters, coffee grinders, and even hair dryers. If anything makes one energy conscious, it's having none.

We've not clocked our wind speed on the ridge yet, but the power is there. Reality kicks in only when considering not just the expense of a turbine but *how.* Short of stabbing one straight down from midair, the logistics of erecting one on the ridge appear impossible. But if it *were* possible, the crest would be the perfect site for a hermitage, a room with a view, a crow's nest, or a tree house (as long as they are topped by lightning rods).

Near Tower, there is an auburn-dark spur of road that leads through sentinel pines to the former site of the fire tower, the one we called "the Tower-tower." As a child, I climbed the tower many times with my father, and I still remember the stomach-churning thrill of bursting up past the tops of pines into clear sky, always windier and warmer than below in summer and always windier and cooler in spring or fall.

My particular vertigo is more physical than mental, my insides gathering into a weird, buzzy clench. I suspect this is genetic since Sam has it, too; on cliffs and bridges he would cling, reporting, "Mommy, my testicles tingle."

Dad pulled me up the tower once to meet the ranger, who must have been a very patient fellow to allow a child into his tiny space, at least patient enough not to toss one over the side. I was obsessed by the tower and afraid of it—it *swayed*. Still, I desperately wanted to live in it. After it was decommissioned, we continued visiting as trespassers, warned by the ominous squeal of rusted bolts.

Forest rangers are rarely if ever set up in metal aeries these days; there are better methods of fire spotting, such as satellite-harvested digital imagery systems like MODIS (Moderate Resolution Imaging Spectroradiometer, of course). DNR planes continue to run observation flights a few times a day when fire danger is high. The local fleet is a trio of vintage de Havilland Beavers built in the late 1950s, painted bobber red and white. When not airborne, they are kept perfectly maintained like thoroughbreds in watery corrals on Shagawa Lake, with new engines installed every so many thousands of flight hours. Occasionally one will skim overhead, making its giant-dragonfly hum, a wing dipped like a nod, reassuring us that even when we are not here, this place is being looked after.

Four

When bonding with a scrap of land, it helps to blaze paths, plant trees, and bury loved ones on it. When Bald Walter finally wore out, he was twenty-three, roughly one hundred and sixty in cat years. He'd just gone blind, and his kidneys were sputtering. On the kitchen scale, he weighed less than four pounds. It was time, and thankfully Sam was either at his dad's or on some overnight. I took Walt to the vet, planning to say good-bye and get it over with in a painless narcotic nod-off to the finish. But the obtuse intern on call wanted to do some tests and keep Walter for observation, certain that with some invasive and expensive medical intervention, he might last another month or so. I blinked at the stupid man, wondering what it was he didn't understand. Unfortunately, it was a Friday night, and our regular vet wouldn't be back until Monday. I took Walt home and made a little nest for him on my bed, then ground up what I thought would be enough valium to kill a large dog and mixed it with cod liver oil and juice from a can of tuna. I fed this Kevorkian cocktail to Walter with a dropper through his chipped, tea-colored teeth while playing old Cat Stevens tunes. In his final hour, Walter's breathing smoothed, and he looked so peaceful, I took one of the leftover valium myself and we both drifted off. In the morning,

I drifted back, damp-mopped Walter's little corpse, and fluffed him with the blow dryer, drying the wet spots I'd bawled onto his fur.

Sam and I laid Walt out in his picnic basket casket just like a real wake, and a few friends came by to pay respects, milling and toasting until they were, as the Irish say, quite full. I wanted to bury Walter on the land and honor his tenacity by planting a tree on top of him, but April in Minnesota is no time to plant anyone. This I'd learned from Dad's sisters, the Aunts, after the last of their five brothers died, inconveniently, in the off-season. The Aunts arranged for Uncle Teddy to be kept in the mortuary cooler until July so that his burial could coincide with their annual vacation to Ely. Ted had not been quite right since coming home from Korea with a metal buckle holding his skull shut, and while he'd been a bit jittery, he was a nice enough fellow. If cold storage was good enough for Uncle Teddy, it was good enough for Walt. I wedged his basket-casket into the freezer under the Skinny Cows and waited for the north to thaw.

In the meantime, I shopped for a tree. What sort would best honor a steadfast, bantamweight runt? In all our years together, Walter never destroyed a piece of upholstery with his fishhook claws, didn't hock up hairballs, and was an adroit bat catcher, saving me the trouble. Even toward the end, he'd made valiant stabs at reaching the litter box, which alone deserved some tribute. And he loved me, meaning he understood that only I could operate the can opener.

I searched local nurseries for a native tree that could tolerate thin, rocky soil and a tundra-like climate. Tamarack seemed most appropriate but was unavailable at Bachman's, so I settled on the next most logical choice, an expensive but lush white pine.

After the thaw, I packed Walt into the car along with a spade, a gallon of water, and the tree, shivering on its side. I slid a cassette of Barber's Agnus Dei in the stereo because Walter loved a good dirge, and we hit the road. Four hours later we bounced up the logging road, the front seat full of wet little balls of tissue, Walt still frozen stiff.

I'd chosen a building site in the high pines at the eastern edge of the land overlooking the little island. At that time, the meandering trail to it was nearly a thousand-foot trek, thick with eye-thwacking alder and difficult enough when empty-handed, but I was carrying a basket of cat, a jug, a spade, and the heavy tree. Barely into the brush, I stopped to rearrange, pulling the still-frozen curlicue of Walter from his basket and fitting him over my forearm like a fur bangle. A spade over one shoulder, a gallon of water in one hand, and the tree perched on my hip, thrashing like a toddler, I tromped over the trail. When I finally breached the clearing with my portable funeral, I shaded my eyes to scope out a decent burial spot. That's when I noticed: if there was one small white pine gracing the vista, there were a hundred.

When "digging" here, one learns quickly not to jab a spade any old place, or the shock will travel arms to shoulders, rattling the skeleton like a cartoon x-ray. Here on the rocky, petered-out end of the Canadian Shield, there's only the slightest lacing of soil, a mere hankie of dirt dropped by the glacier. Terry came over to help. He was on the patch again and tense. About twice a month, he would make the motions to quit smoking but never got farther than wearing the patch until he wanted a cigarette, when he simply tore it off. After much scraping and cursing, there was finally a hole just big enough for a stiff little cat and a few strands of white pine root.

I made a mental note to add "Please cremate" to my half-completed, unregistered will somewhere in the folder labeled DEAD.

Even with no portable funeral to carry, just getting to my site was a hump. Having chosen the most remote plateau at the far eastern edge of the property, I had effectively rendered myself end-of-the-road inaccessible. I'd have my privacy but I would need a long driveway, a real road. I invited three excavators out to bid.

After years of renovating houses and dealing daily with contractors, one learns what signs to watch for. The first guy showed up with manicured hands clean enough to excavate teeth with. His truck was waxed and undented, his feet shod in shoes, not boots. He obviously didn't do any of the work himself and advertised his business as the only environment-friendly road builder in the area, yet when asked what that meant, he only mumbled. Perhaps assuming because I was female and therefore possibly gullible and maybe, hopefully gouge-able because of my 612 area code, he came in with a bid that was double the average.

The lowest bid was from a man who barely looked at the site as he walked along next to me, extolling the quality of his work with such a tone of desperation I wondered when he'd start tugging my sleeve. When he insisted he could start the next *day*, I figured there was some reason he was so wildly available and so cheap.

The middle bid came from a guy I'll call Chim, who already had more work than he could handle and had only come out reluctantly. Breaking through brush alongside him, I was impressed by his grousing. He pointed out various obstacles, a particularly large tree, the difficulty, how he would have to approach this dip or that curve or move an immovable boulder. When we had walked the length, I asked if he wanted to measure the distance on the way back.

"Already have," he replied. "Seven-hundred seventy-five feet, give or take a few." The whole time we'd been talking and tromping, he'd been counting his steps in a measured stride. I already knew he was busy and didn't need the work, and his truck was filthy, so I wanted him. My only advantage was that I was in no hurry. I asked if he might pencil me in as his very last job of the season. That way he'd have no next job making him rush through mine. My road wouldn't be something he was squeezing in.

There are as many ways to build a road as there are roads. When milestone birthdays for me and my sister Mary rolled around, she treated me to a vacation in Peru, where we learned that real road construction is not for wimps. The Inca Trail system is the road to end all roads, the difficulty factor eclipsing anything the pantywaist Romans ever built. Most everyone has seen images of Machu Picchu or the walls of Cuzco or Ollantaytambo, just a few examples of stonework the Incas are famous for. To see them up close is something, but what you cannot see is that the impossibly large blocks, sized from shipping crate to small room, are carved on the five set sides with precisely engineered Lego-like indentations and protrusions, one interlocking perfectly with the next. Designed to be earthquake proof, they have remained in place for centuries. In severe quakes, the stones will rattle and dance, only to settle back down just as they were, so tight that a knife blade cannot breach the spaces between. And since the examples of stone walls are so amazing, it's no wonder visitors are too busy looking up to much notice what's underfoot. The roads made a great impression even before I'd learned the Inca didn't yet have the *wheel* at the peak of their building. Until they built roads, there was no place level or flat enough to roll anything. Nor did they have draft animals; horses didn't arrive until the Spaniards imported them along with disease and priests. To build their roads, the Incas were equipped with cleverness, levers, brute strength, and the balance of mountain goats. Theories, equations, and scale models have been constructed in hopes of figuring how they actually did it (besides a whole lot of hernia-popping heave-ho-ing), but those theories mostly fall short and leave modern-day engineers still scratching their heads. Only when the intangible is factored in does it seem possible. An amazing collective of ingenuity, engineering, craftsmanship, and labor would have been nothing without the one factor nonexistent in modern-day construction, *patience.*

For practical purposes and ease of maintenance, Chim usually builds his roads wide, straight, and level from points A to B. I was more inclined to allow the landscape to determine the course of my road and let it wind, since every charming road I'd ever traveled seemed to do just that. Besides, we wouldn't be having the road plowed. This plan was just fine with Chim since it meant less gravel to haul, and it allowed him to avoid difficult boulders and large trees. Curving around them would mean less labor.

In the autumn, when Chim and the boys came, I made sure to be around as a visible presence, even if I was just a distant figure clearing brush. Best the boys see I had a face and wasn't just

The Wallet. In town one evening, I recognized a number of their pickups outside the Portage. I went in to meet the young men I'd only waved at and, not above ingratiating myself, bought a round of drinks none of them needed.

Years ago, while renovating a house during a heat wave, I needed to motivate a crew of stoned, over-warm house painters. I thought about what *I* would want if stuck on a scaffold for the month of July. I doled out popsicles at regular intervals and tuned the radio to an eighties rock station, cranking the volume. I ran the sprinkler during their many breaks. In the end, their paint job was excellent. A few years later, I read of a study wherein subjects were given simple tasks to do while under the influence of separate substances: alcohol, coffee, a placebo, and marijuana. One task, in fact, was painting. The group given alcohol was slow and downright sloppy; the caffeine group was jittery and sloppy. But the stoned group was the most focused and the neatest, outperforming even the placebo group under the influence of *nothing.* The spring after the house was painted, a souvenir cropped up in the shape of a bushy cannabis plant growing just where the scaffolding had been.

Chim's boys were hard workers and needed little more encouragement than a thumbs-up and wave when I passed by. The road took shape, rocks were piled, the layers of gravel spread and tamped. True to the promise they'd made after a third round at the Portage, they did a damn good job, even taking extra care to clear every bit of the debris and smooth out any ruts. They even raked so that I hesitated on my first steps down the road, as if not wanting to sully a Zen garden.

I walked the length of the road five times, all slopes and curves, narrow and shaded. A real cabin road. Still, it had a tenuous feel.

This smooth ribbon of earth, if left untrammeled for a decade or two, would easily close back in on itself, with trees falling, saplings sprouting, and brush growing quick as kudzu—nature prevailing.

I can no longer locate Walter's grave. The little funeral pine died shortly after being planted, perhaps an example that transplants might think twice before just showing up here.

Of course, there are plenty of other trees. One reason I'd been drawn to my building site was that it was shaded by one of the few majestic trees edging the bluff, a giant white pine casting a generous canopy of shelter, its straight arms reaching so far they would shield the roof of the cabin I hoped to build thirty or so feet from its trunk.

After a storm during the second spring, I got word from our neighbor to the east: bad news—my tree of trees had been struck by lightning and had toppled. It had been so tall, the tip of it had crashed over the property line onto the neighbors' land so that, in addition to the loss of that tree and the several it took in its path, I suffered the sting of paying several hundred dollars for a logger to saw up the trunk and clear the mess.

Another giant pine centers our acres, shouldering above the forest. I keep intending to measure it one of these days with the old logger's trick of comparing the length of a tree's shadow to the shadow of the person measuring. First, on a sunny day, stand next to the trunk, then measure the length of your shadow from tip of shoes to top of head (best accomplished with assistance or a metal retractable tape). Walk the length of the tree's shadow from base to tip, measuring as you go. Ideally, the tree you are measuring is the only one growing from the middle of a surface that is soccer-field smooth and perfectly level. Multiply the length of the tree's shadow by your height, and then divide the resulting number by the length of your shadow. Got that? So if you're five feet tall, your shadow is eight feet long, and the tree's shadow is one hundred feet long, the height of the tree is $(100 \times 5) / 8 = 62.5$ feet. In the meantime, I'll just claim the white pine is, like, super tall.

We explored, poking around in mossy low spots and climbing slopes that left us panting. Deciding on sites for our respective cabins was a leisurely process since neither Terry, Susan, nor I had means to build anything in the beginning. Eventually we settled on two sites that by chance lie on opposite boundaries of the parcels. Both are high and set back, just far enough to comply with the requisite building codes. Between us are the beaver valley, the piney plateau, and the bog; you cannot see one site from the other. The terrain is so rugged, so up and down and pocked with old blast holes, depressions, and sheer drops that if our acres were ironed flat, we reckon we'd have a hundred.

It seemed little had happened on the land—not much evidence anyone besides Bog Man had ever inhabited the place, or even much roamed it, though we can assume fur traders, Dakota, and Ojibwe had passed through or even camped here. A trail of pin oaks suggests they had, so we have every hope of one day finding a real arrowhead. In the meantime, I've considered buying and planting a few so that one day when I'm dotty and I've forgotten, I might have the thrill of discovering one.

For centuries, the area was dominated by white pine, which were logged out so long ago even stumps of the original forest have rotted or burned away. Almost no old-growth pine survived logging, save a stand northeast of town on Hegman Lake and, much farther west, a legendary forest called the Lost Forty near Big Falls. The Lost Forty is technically the Lost One Hundred Forty, a sort of primeval wonderland that only stands today because a clerical gaffe botched the sale of its stumpage (timber parcels were called "stumpage" even before they were logged, in a descriptive preview of the end result).

Along our shore, the white pines are now counted in the hundreds rather than thousands. The few old-growth survivors are stunning and obvious in the landscape, breaking out above the forest canopy here and there with the fanfare of a stripper bursting from a cake. Many of the bases of these old dames are scarred by fire, and with their wide-reaching arms, they make broad targets for lightning. The tops are often sheared, leaving their upper branches curved skyward like cupped hands, as if waiting patiently to be handed back their missing crowns or to accept a spot of rain. There is plentiful red pine, less majestic, most sixty to eighty or so years old, foot soldiers risen in the ranks after the tail end of the logging. The red pine jockey for space with the poplar and thick alder that make most of our acreage impassable. Two hundred years ago, this was a primeval temple of pine corridors lit by beams sifting between the sturdy fretwork of limbs, the sky only glitter above the forest canopy. Living among such sentinel trees as the natives and early settlers did must have imbued a sense of awe and security, or claustrophobia. John Muir wrote, "Between every two pines is a doorway to a new world," a whimsical musing, and one I think of when transplanting fledgling pines or heading out with a saw or loppers to encourage the existing young by clearing space around them. There are countless clusters of three or four young pines growing too close together for success, so I cut the stragglers that the hardiest might thrive. Cutting pine saplings feels a little like mowing down kindergartners, but I have less hesitation when whacking a birch or poplar crowding a pine. Bloodlust takes over when I'm confronted with American green alder, the vermin tree that exists solely to spite me. As random and disorganized as my micro–forest management is, it may one day result in a bit more piney shade and needle orange ground for Sam's kids and grandkids to play on; at least that's what I tell myself while sweating and chopping and sawing and lopping.

Since Walter's burial, two more cats have found their final resting places here, Nutty and Lazzie, longtime companions to Terry and Susan. Those pets also had trees planted for them, but both were cremated, their nuggety bits of bone strewn like cat seeds.

Five

Once the road was finished, I could drive to my site and sit
rather than break trail to my site and sit. The plateau is situated high on the north side of the lake, a span of needle orange
ground with round outcroppings of granite fringe spilling over its
rim like beer foam. I balanced a garden bench on a ledge where
a front porch might one day be and admired the view.

But one can only sit for so long.

The site was looking untidy. There was nowhere to put the
pickaxes and pry bars and loppers, so I bought a heavy Rubber-
maid coffin that would at least keep a few things dry and keep
blades from rusting. Each trip from home, I brought a few more
items so that the clearing slowly filled with birdhouses, hammocks, trash barrels, benches, lawn chairs, crates, water jugs, bird
feeders, shovels, rakes, hoes, saws, tarps, everything but the yard
gnome. When the clearing began to resemble a yard sale, I saw I
could no longer put off building or buying a shed.

I'd noticed an ad in the local paper for sheds and playhouses.
An older man, Rory, answered the phone. Rory eagerly talked up
the unusual little structures he'd advertised without actually telling me how or what they were made of, just that they were very
handsome sheds and "not for everyone," so I probably wouldn't

even want one, but maybe I'd like to come out and look anyway. A lot of people, apparently, went out to look. He claimed these were "some of the sturdiest little sheds ever built; you just don't see 'em *built* like this anymore." Rory added that his son could build anything, and only then did I ascertain that the son, Lars, was the man I needed to talk to. Rory said Lars also built small cabins that were, again, probably not for everyone, leaving me to wonder what the hell was wrong with them. Were they geodesic domes? A-frames? Made of pressboard? Yurts?

"Oh, no," Rory assured me. "These here are built like brick shithouses."

"They're brick?"

"Ha! No."

"So," I ventured, "then they must be sh— ?"

"Ha! Good one." Rory's guffaw was a little like Goofy's. I finally pried it out of him that they were timber, "not timber-*frame* timber, but timber *log*, but not round log, more like square, and not like those little sheds for sale on roadsides with the fake log siding from Menards, either, but the *real thing*." It took fifteen more minutes to ascertain that Rory's son could indeed make me a shed but wasn't able to come to the phone just then because he was "probly out dragging timber."

I'd learned from the boys at the Portage that there are up-north euphemisms for nearly every bodily function, sexual pastime, and anatomical feature, from "wedding tackle" for male genitalia to "mud badger" for homosexual. When Rory said "dragging timber," disturbing images from masturbation to nose-picking flitted through my mind, but Rory assured me Lars was literally dragging timber. It turned out he had a permit to pull blowdown trees from the Boundary Waters, eighty-foot red and white pine toppled in the '99 storm that were now curing where they fell, threatening to become tinder for the mother of all forest fires. Because of the fire threat, temporary exceptions were made to the ban on motorized traffic within the park, and logging equipment was allowed in the few places that could be breached. These logs weren't just fallen trees; these were prime old-growth timber, a hundred-plus years old, the sort of log that would give a logger a woody.

Rory explained Lars had his own sawmill, that he cut his own timber, milled it, and built his square-log structures from it, reviving the traditional method of dovetailed cornering. He did it all the old way.

"Finnish style?" I asked, suddenly intrigued.

"Swedish, Finnish, whatever you want."

I said I'd come look, though I probably couldn't afford what he was describing. The buildings sounded like the type of structures that my father and I had sometimes encountered on our tromps through the countryside while hunting for insulators. Lars's buildings sounded like old homesteads my father called Finlander farms.

Dad retired when I was a teen and, either bored or just not that imaginative, took to his new hobby like a man possessed, collecting old glass and ceramic insulators from decommissioned electrical poles. Insulators, if you've never seen one, are made in a variety of shapes and colors and are utterly useless beyond their original function—too round-bottomed to be flipped and used as ashtrays or pencil holders, and not heavy enough to be bookends or doorstops. Mostly they were just clutter lining the windowsills, sending colored rays across every surface so that on sunny mornings we sat down to blue and green cornflakes. As an object they're pretty lame, but then the object wasn't the object, I eventually realized. The *hunt* for the object and what it entailed held all the appeal—a perfect excuse for Dad to meander the countryside, scavenging ditches and defunct rail beds, sticking his head into abandoned places along washboard dirt roads winding through rural nowhere. I went along for no other reason than that I was learning to drive and could do the least amount of damage on back roads. At worst I might startle a deer while tearing along at fifteen miles per hour.

These areas were so remote I couldn't fathom why there were even telephone poles in the first place. The answer came in the shells of deserted clapboard houses and barns stove in as if stomped, rock farms where a successful crop of potatoes would have been considered a triumph. Most farms were eventually abandoned because even a bumper crop of Minnesota potatoes wasn't enough to support a family, and the soil wasn't fit for much else. Most homesteaders had given in by the forties, done in by the Depression, the climate, futility, or all three. We rarely bothered going into these clapboard houses, for all held the same contents: reeking mattresses, porn, broken glass, and beer cans from every vintage representing every high school class between '38 and '73, the year sometimes smeared onto the wall in senior feces.

More remote jaunts brought us to the Finnish farms, when Dad would grow suddenly alert the way he would whenever Joan Embery from the San Diego Zoo was on *The Tonight Show* with some terrified primate stuck to her thigh or clutching her khaki boobs. To me, these homesteads were just more crappy old buildings in high grass mined with glass, boards riddled with nails, and potential for more tetanus shots. Most of the buildings had never been painted and had weathered in shades of gray from driftwood to charcoal. Some still had cedar-shake roofs, usually with saplings or moss growing on them. Others stood like open boxes. We climbed and crawled around in lofts of old barns and houses stripped of everything but their heavy sinks or rusty stoves with birds nesting in the flues. We ducked into windowless sauna buildings with blackened interiors as inviting as any in *The Count of Monte Cristo.* Saunas, Dad informed me, were where most Finn women went to have their babies. Right, I thought, looking around at the hard benches and charred walls, as if you'd leave your bed in a house to come *here* to do *that.* He told me entire families would often sauna together, slapping each other with birch whips, rinsing each other with buckets of melted snow. The thought of naked brothers or even sisters was enough to send Tab rushing back up my throat, but a father—*naked?*

Since Dad spoke so little, I tended to listen when he bothered, and he did go on about the construction of these spare old buildings, pointing out the intricately dovetailed corners, describing how they were cut and fit. Most were made of pine, but a few were cedar. Once we found a small shed that looked dainty for its 4x4-inch timbers, but Dad determined it was tamarack and said it was dense as hell, assuring me the little building would still be standing long after he and I had rotted in the ground.

He showed me the difference between simple log joinery—full lap and half lap and dovetail notches, or Finnish notches. Simple joinery would suffice, but dovetail or Finnish notches kept the logs from twisting, providing the tensile qualities of full lap, the flush corners of half lap, and the strength of both. To me it all seemed like just more labor in an already laborious process, but Dad explained that certain cultures at certain latitudes, like the Finns, have a dearth of sunlight and not a whole lot to do all winter except drink or find more ways to make work for themselves.

I mentioned to Rory that I might stop by Lars's sawmill next time I was in his neighborhood—seventy miles away—to check out his sheds and meet him. I waited twenty-four hours so as not to seem overeager.

The sawmill sat a few miles inland from Lake Superior. Scattered across the lot were sawn planks stacked to dry, a smattering of buildings, and a fence of old cars sunk into the weeds. A big-toothed lab sprouted from nowhere to snarl and slobber on my window, barking until a man came out from a building, also barking, woofing and clapping with sawdust rising from his shoulders with each gesture. I only hoped he was calling the dog.

Lars didn't look much like a logger. For starters he was a little guy, one of those dark Scandinavians with slightly impish, elfish features, like Bjork. As if to compensate, his gravelly voice was a broad, pitch-perfect match to that of Canadian hip-hopper Buck 65, whose songs portray life at the rural fringes with lyrics that are so much more excellent than his titles "Sick Stew," "Jaws of Life," or "Cat Piss." Lars spoke in the local vernacular of double negatives with a thrift that truncated what few words he spoke. He gave me a tour of the little buildings. There were several outhouses and saunas, solid and hobbity looking, a few with whimsical details and all almost comically overbuilt with eight- and ten-inch-square logs. The joinery was dovetail, with Lars's signature flair of a two-inch bump-out and his added finishing touch: a bevel on each facet edge of each log, including the dovetail. In fact, the edges of every piece of wood or fascia board on Lars's buildings were beveled, which meant that for each single log or board milled, Lars made *twelve additional* bevel cuts. The same was true for every trim board, doorjamb, or shutter, which would have kept Lars busy all winter, surely too busy to become a raging drunk. I asked after the outhouses, which he admitted *might* be for sale, as if he wasn't sure and would have to check with himself.

There were two larger old homestead buildings Lars had salvaged and reconstructed, each log numbered and marked. These Swede houses, as Lars called them, would have been bulldozed had he not spotted and nabbed them. Apparently many such buildings across the region have been lost over time, many probably never even identified but covered over in siding or, worse, razed and used for garden beds or firewood.

Lars showed me his white pine logs waiting to be milled into 8 × 8-inch and 10 × 10-inch beams, densely grained, with ends revealing almost no space between the growth rings, indicating just how long it took them to reach such great heights. I thought of my flight with Mel, seeing the swaths of these downed giants, most fallen in places far too remote to ever salvage. What Lars and others had gleaned was pitiful in comparison, a handful of matchsticks from a barrel. The notion of something new, something useful arising from the result of devastation, appealed to me. What might have been a natural event for the forest was tragic for canoeists and campers, but in these buildings, the loss would at least come to something—outhouses or saunas that would stand for longer than it takes to grow another eighty-foot pine. While it would take a few tense years and several forest fires before the all-clear could be sounded in the Boundary Waters, it will take a century for the lost pines to come back.

I'd gone to the sawmill to poke around in sheds I probably couldn't afford but was surprised when Lars finally named a price for the smallest, plainest structure. They were reasonable, he explained, because there was no middleman. He was the logger, sawyer, architect, and builder. I could practically feel Dad's breath in my ear. "Now we're talkin', Sally."

"Architect" was a stretch, but I was sold, if only to stop Dad from swinging on my earlobe with his tinny mantra of "Do it!" Did it matter that this whole project was beginning to feel steered by desires not quite my own? I do not believe in an afterlife from which the dead harass or heckle us, but I did embark on my quest with my father plainly in mind, spurred by memory, hoping to bridge the missed connection between him and Sam, grandfather and grandson, a generation skipped like a very long pause between heartbeats. Though I was alone in it, I'd set about obtaining a place for us *all*, and I went to work with a vision of the kind of place that my father would have loved and that Sam would hopefully come to love and bond with, a place that would one day be his legacy, whether he wanted it or not.

Several years before, I'd walked around Tower with Sam, showing him the cemetery, the building where my grandfather's tailor shop once was, and the white house by the creek where Dad and his brothers and sisters were raised. We climbed the steep hill leading away from town on a wooded trail. Sam scooted ahead of me to walk backwards uphill. "Tell me another story about Grandpa."

I was already hoarse from telling and out of breath. "*One* more." I told him about Margaret, the cat I brought home a year or so before Dad died.

Dad took one look at her and said, "No. No way. No cats."

"Okay." I shrugged. Margaret was long-haired and gray with a distinct half-white face and white paws. "I'll bring her back to the animal shelter on the weekend."

The next day when I got home from my shift at the hardware store, Dad was on the floor, having woven a six-foot sling of rubber bands with a heavy knot of hemp rope attached to its middle, the whole contraption suspended from the arch separating the living room from the dining room. "Watch this." He rolled to his back and launched the knot to the next room where teeny Margaret was perched on a chair, waiting. When the knot came at her like a wrecking ball, she pounced and dug her needle claws in. Since she weighed only ounces, the bungee action zinged her into the living room and back again—living room, dining room, living room, dining room—clinging as if to a comet hurtling through space. Dad was beside himself.

"Don't worry," I reminded him. "I'll have her out of here by Saturday."

By Thursday, he was hand-feeding her thawed tidbits from his stash of frozen walleye cheeks. He shook a little bag of what looked to me like weed. "It's true about catnip," he informed me. "Look at her. She's completely, what do you call it . . . *baked?*"

I leaned on the door frame. "*She* is?"

My plan was working nicely. Dad fell asleep to Johnny Carson's closing theme with Margaret buttoned into his sweater vest. On Friday, I came home to him stapling carpet remnants around the posts of a Realtor's for-sale sign with its bottom still muddy, building a hideous scratching post. "Don't get too attached," I reminded him. But when I got up on Saturday, he'd already spirited Margaret away on his weekend rounds to rummage sales and to my sister's house for coffee.

Margaret loved the car as a dog does, especially the back window, becoming Dad's own furry mascot. He started taking her to the cabin. They slept together.

"Did Grandpa hate cats?" Sam asked.

"Mostly," I said. Just then a large rabbit jumped onto the path ahead, and we froze in our tracks. It didn't move. We inched closer. It wasn't a jackrabbit or ratty wood rabbit but a big, glossy Alice in Wonderland rabbit. It stood on its back legs and stared at us as if it had been waiting. I half expected it to take out a pocket watch.

Sam looked at the rabbit. The rabbit looked at him. Sam petted the rabbit and looked at me in awe, whispering, "Maybe it's Grandpa?" Lately he'd been puzzling over the mysteries of life and seemed to come home every day with a new question about being or not being and what makes alive alive and dead dead. He had a cardboard contraption he'd made called the Death Machine in which he placed stuffed animals he had "made dead," but then, after a lot of sound effects and fiddling with buttons magic markered onto the box, they miraculously came back to life—Sam at the helm, of course. He was frequently babysat by a family who were Bible-thumping fundamentalists, and while I'd asked that any reading there be limited to Dr. Seuss and Sam's *Fun with Science!* books, who knew what tales of resurrections and afterlife he was regaled with over cookies and milk?

"Grandpa?" I could guess where he might be going with this, and indeed the rabbit wasn't your Average Rabbit. He was tended and tame and probably someone's escaped or abandoned pet. Circling the rabbit, I looked for a tag or collar (collar, on a rabbit?). Just as I reached out for him, he bounded away, saving me from trying to figure out how to capture it *and* what to do with it.

"Well, wouldn't it be neat if it *was* Grandpa?" I shrugged. "*But . . .*" We had a four-hour car ride ahead of us, plenty of time to go over the final finality of life. I'd been raised in a faith that dangled the carrot of an afterlife while at the same time instilling such fear for this one that, at Sam's age, I'd assumed guardian angels were snitches and that I was doomed to fry. Early on in motherhood, I'd determined he'd have a secular upbringing with "just the facts." I'd already watched my mother, at the end of a life not well lived, grasp for a last straw by suddenly reembracing the church that had excommunicated her to ask for the Last Rites, hoping for a bus ticket to somewhere beyond the end of the line.

And as great as it would be to imagine my son and father meeting up to go fishing on some everlasting lake, I could provide something tangible by giving Sam some place his grandfather would have liked to provide himself: a cabin in the woods, however modest, a real place set in the actual kingdom of nature.

↬

Between our scratchings on a yellow legal pad, Lars and I worked up a few designs, one for an outhouse similar to one in the lumberyard and another for a small "starter" cabin of just 10 × 12 feet with a sleeping loft. Tiny, but enough for the moment, and hopefully down the road I would be able to afford to have Lars build something larger, when the small cabin could become my studio. I wrote a check for a deposit.

Once back at the site, I looked around at the clutter of water jugs and folded lawn chairs and realized: I still didn't have a shed.

Six

We owned the land three years before Lars went to work on the starter cabin. Until then, I'd somehow shrugged off consequences of being so far off the grid. "Pristine, undeveloped" is how the mining company had listed it, and during the heady time of finding and buying (as if medicated), that description had an almost whimsical ring to it, like a Disneyesque glade populated by Bambi and fairies on pink toadstools and affectionate wolves. Had one been rational at that time, one might have looked into just what "undeveloped" meant in the way of expenses down the road. "Road" being just one. The driveway had already chomped off far more than its allotted share of what I casually called the "budget," which in reality was my retirement.

No road access, water, septic, or electricity. Just how much I'd bitten off became clear when I called around to price getting hooked up. Power from the grid a mile and a half away required erecting poles every three hundred feet, and since it's impossible to plant poles *in* the ground here, much drilling into ledge rock is necessary to hold them upright by way of angle irons, raising the cost to sixteen hundred dollars per pole in addition to the ten dollars per foot for the line itself, adding up to over $40k, which explained why the clerk at the power company had been so sympathetic. Solar was the only option. And since sun is not an everyday occurrence around here, panels would need to be supplemented with a generator or wind turbine should we ever want to power more than lights.

Drilling wells here is hysterically expensive, which should have come as no surprise given the terrain: all bedrock, often requiring hydrofracking, a technique borrowed from iron mining to augment traditional drilling. If no water is forthcoming at a depth of, say, five hundred or more feet of drilling, the hole is blasted with enough water pressure to break into horizontal aquifers or cracks harboring water. A someday flush toilet would require mounded septic, costing yet another small fortune. Pumps for such things as wells and septic need electricity, so you can't really have one without the other. Necessities turned out to be luxuries beyond reach

Ironically, high-speed wireless Internet *is* available, with a tower so near we can see its lights blinking just over the ridge. Great, should I ever want to surf Facebook by lantern light during my ever-dwindling laptop battery hours.

I stopped by the sawmill to see progress on the cabin. The square logs had been notched and the walls built up to armpit height. The freshly milled wood was the color of September hay, and the structure stood in its own little yard of drifted, wonderful-smelling sawdust. I climbed over a wall and stood inside and realized I had made a grave mistake.

Even with no roof, it seemed claustrophobic, no larger than a Finnish henhouse. Lars assured me it only *felt* small because there were no windows yet and it was empty. I'd asked for small, hadn't I?

I could do without power or water, I realized, if only there was just enough *space*. At least room enough so no one goes mad after a few days of rain. Space for a couch and a comfy chair for reading, a wall for bookshelves, a room with a door to close for naps and privacy, a porch with a table just for cribbage and jigsaw puzzles that needn't be cleared each mealtime. What I really should have had Lars build was a little cabin, a modest six to eight hundred square feet. What I'd commissioned was a playhouse.

Or maybe I should have just started with the most important room of any cabin and built the screened porch first in hopes of tacking on a cabin later. I once lived in the countryside outside of Duluth on a road that sported two "starter homes": basements that had been topped and capped with tarpaper, with enclosed staircases reaching up from below as if groping for rooms that weren't there. For as long as I lived on that road, neither basement ever sprouted a house. The subterranean families continued to live like earthworms with only glass-block chunks of daylight. The mailbox outside of one was lettered "The Glooms." If whole families of Glooms could live in basements, I could make do in a porch.

Small is good; it's sustainable. Small is smart, but tiny is more of a challenge.

The bungalow generation of architects seemed to get it most right about how we live in our spaces, not least by acknowledging the duck-and-cover instinct humans have, designing smallish rooms to host an occupant without dwarfing them, acknowledging that, as bipeds, we move side to side but do not shoot up into the air, a fact lost on 1980s builders so fond of great rooms with soaring ceilings. After renovation of the old Victorian that

Sam was raised in, his bedroom had fresh white walls, gleaming woodwork, and windows flooding light over the newly varnished floor—an airy, generous space. Yet come bedtime, Sam would pad down the hall to the tiny guest room, a cozy box with thick carpet and walls tinted a rusty mauve that on a paint chip might have been called "womb."

Big cabins are just wrong, and big-*big* cabins are crimes upon the landscape, but we would need a *little* more than the log box I was standing in. I sat with Lars, and we designed a second building to be used for storage. It would be slightly smaller at 8 × 11 and timber-frame, so less expensive. It could be built more quickly. In fact, Lars said he could put it up within a few months. I decided on a spot just east of the driveway.

The timbers went up fast, and once the bones of the building were erect, I realized it was far too nice for storage. As living space, it would have just enough room for a bed and a chamber pot to slide under it. Lars's dad, Rory, was recruited to finish the building. Since there was no money for much more than the basics, I was informed I had to decide between a roof and windows. I gave up windows and opted for screens all around, with a three-foot-high skirting of cedar shake around the bottom, making it a sort of sleeping porch.

Once built, it looked exactly like a fish house, so the name stuck. Since it was conceived only as a storage shed, it wasn't the tightest building, with countless thoroughfares in and out for the mice and bugs of all orders. During its first years of use, I was constantly plugging cracks with spray foam, steel wool, and logger's caulk, sometimes with odd results. When the hard-to-control spray foam shot right through a gap to the outside, I went out to check under the eaves to find a perfectly scaled male member hardened in foam, pointing west.

Still, mice owned the place, sprinting maniacally across the framework of beams as if it were a Habitrail custom built for them. Eventually, I would give in and drape mosquito netting over the bed, at least to keep mouse turds from falling directly onto sleeping heads and wolf spiders from crawling into bed. With netting, one snoring with mouth agape would only inhale the tiniest of moths, and insects crawling into ears would be of the petite variety. Most everyone here knows the trick for getting a bug out of an ear, but every now and again a tourist will be spotted whacking his head like a swimmer or unmedicated schizophrenic, at least until someone takes pity and drags them into some dark toilet to use their cell phone light to coax the thing out.

Considering what little amount of living space we would have, one of my mother's axioms came back to me: "There is a place for everything, and everything has its place." We would have to take care to put things away, keep tables clear, keep shoes and boots off the floor, and have nothing inside that doesn't belong or have some vital function. Maybe I also suffer her "see chaos, feel chaos" aversion that prevents me from feeling good in any place cluttered. There really wouldn't be any place to store things since, once again, we didn't have a shed.

Out of sight but not out of mind is my cabin hope chest, a former Mayflower moving van parked in a lot near Ely where it sits chockablock among a hundred others, all retired and repurposed and rented as storage. With its crisp grass and gravel alleys, the place has a desultory air, an abandoned place of abandoned things. Situated as it is next to the college, it's the perfect choice for a hazing or a kegger. Driving in, I skirt a few pole barns and sheds and a trailer Jed Clampett might have dragged behind his jalopy, its wooden sides weighted with a dozen vintage outboard motors like sailors clamped to a raft. When a breeze kicks up, a few propellers turn, and I step on it, imagining the old Johnsons and Neptunes all coughing to life at once to propel themselves after me into the maze of trailers.

At the end of the lane is an odd brick building worthy of a double take, its architecture slightly Gothic with a round stained-glass window in its peak, an old Masonic Temple or Odd Fellows Hall (men used to be odder). The building was impressive once, but isolated as it is and misplaced in the middle of storageland, it is doubly creepy. I wonder what's inside yet don't really want to know. Number 90 is my trailer, and I've never found it on the first try, usually twining a few times down lanes of cabless trailers with faded logos for Gateway or Monson. If the tires weren't all flat, I'd swear the owner moves them around for fun. Number 90 is plain white, its sides painted over. All that stands between potential thieves and the treasures inside is a padlock the size found on diaries, weak enough to be bitten through.

By "treasure," I mean the old crap people's parents had the sense to get rid of when they could afford better: former rumpus-room rejects that have become the furnishings of our future summers, all carefully collected over decades and chosen to evoke an era when cabins were cabins.

I don't know much about how other fathers and daughters bonded, but Dad and I got solid at rummage sales and junk shops. We developed a code and were often in collusion, able to remain calm and stony faced when chancing upon the rare sale or item priced to reveal that the seller was clueless. I once found a pair of deco garnet earrings set in gold amid the chain-snarl junk of a jewelry box marked twenty-five cents. In the car, Dad gave me high fives for not grinning like an idiot while paying for them. We would hold things up for each other to scrutinize across tables cluttered with castoffs, and a slight nod or a frown meant you either had a prize or you didn't. I picked up a pair of petite metal dumbbells and pondered aloud, "Steel dumbbells?" to Dad's droll response, "Leave here."

What's in the trailer is just stuff, but it somehow represents possibility because once these items are finally in place, they will mark the end of many years of pining for a cabin. It's easy to forget what's there, so that a trip down the thirty-two-foot aisle can feel like Christmas. Plastic tubs hold old linens and woolen striped blankets layered with cedar shakes to thwart moths. Juice glasses with painted stripes or 1960s cartoon characters are stacked next to a box of money-colored souvenir plates from thirty different states (in case that many happen to drop by for dinner). Against one wall is a massive cast-iron kitchen sink with a high apron and two deep basins and drain boards, salvaged from a Cass Gilbert house in St. Paul, a steal at "free for the taking!" until I realized the taking would take four men. Another old sink from a house I renovated awaits some future bathroom, along with a set of wooden medicine chests.

There are minnow buckets with leaping-fish logos, a 1920s camp stove, railroad spikes, thick Tuco puzzles of seascapes and hunting scenes, cribbage boards, old playing cards with scenes of pointer dogs and mallards, Chinese checkers, Scrabble, and heavy poker chips in a rotating caddy. Several boxes hold framed paint-by-number wildlifes and woodland vistas, sometimes signed. Grandpa-tools and oil cans, orange crates, a humidor, and a collection of table lamps not lit since the Korean War. The trailer is packed with thirty years' worth of haunting alleys, thrift shops, rummage sales, and flea markets. Along the way were many "ah hahs!", or "You're throwing that out?", or "Would you take three dollars?" There are enough pots and pans, canisters, melamine dishware, Fire-King bowls, and spattered enamelware to stock two kitchens, plus full sets of cutlery and utensils in Bakelite and a carving set with antler handles. The heaviest boxes are on the bottom, holding cast-iron skillets I may be too old and weak to lift by the time there is a kitchen to hang them in. Chairs and occasional tables painted in glossy yesteryear colors of dull mustard, forest service green, and robin's egg blue. Cowboy bedspreads, Indian blankets, a seven-piece suite of rattan rumpus-room furniture, and a box of Ed Sullivan–era bark-cloth drapes to reupholster the cushions with. Part of the rattan ensemble was scored in my St. Paul alley one morning on my way to an important interview. I was already late when I saw the near-perfect set but certain that if I didn't act, it would be gone in an hour. Mincing along in high heels, I dragged each piece down the icy ruts to my garage.

I wasn't the only dumpster diver in my neighborhood. Regular pickers in ratty trucks and vans cruised the alleys, some on bikes pulling little trailers piled high with aluminum cans. A few came on foot. A fellow diver, Paul Wellstone, lived just a few streets over. I'd encountered him a number of times in his red running shorts (a convenient ruse), usually in the evenings. Our neighborhood had great potential for found treasure since there seemed always to be a house or two in the throes of renovation, with big roll-off dumpsters in their driveways that by end of day were often loaded. Clutching a garish lamp or carrying a plywood magazine rack or light fixture salvaged from the trash, the Senator and I would greet each other shyly and go our separate ways, dragging our prizes.

A box marked "Wooden Things" is loaded with mass-produced tourist kitsch once sold in dime stores and gas stations across America, specific to the place only by the cheap ink stampings that read "Niagara Falls" or "Mount Hood." Wall plaques, little boxes, salt and pepper shakers, etc., all in varnished cedar or diamond willow. A few Wooden Things are actually homemade, no doubt by dead grandfathers or shop class juniors, for who else would make an agate-crusted tissue box cover, a trivet with a wood-burned portrait of a pug named Ruffian, or amateurish Bambi bookends with glued-on googly eyes? Many of the items have bits of history tacked on, and pawing through, I sometimes daydream little vignettes. The set of never-used embroidered tea towels might have been a gift to some sturdy blond bride, but Inga or Astrid would've been too practical to ever use something so nice, stowing them to be saved for "good." Either good never came or they were forgotten because come time for the nursing home, closets were emptied, and now the towels are mine. I can imagine a mod mom in pedal pushers filling the old plaid pitcher thermos with Kool-Aid, her hair teased and her pastel aluminum juice glass jazzed with vodka. Or a crew-cut Dad in a madras plaid shirt at the tiki bar ashing his Parliament onto the ceramic stomach of an ashtray shaped like a hula dancer with big ones.

Some things have real stories and meaning, like my Grandmother Julia's rocking chair, which I stripped of paint with toxic goo and dental tools to reveal intricate carved irises. I also have a vintage White sewing machine from Grandpa Joe's tailor shop. I'm not sure how these items landed with me, but I suspect the Aunts were grateful for the time I stayed in Ely for half a February with Grandma Julia after she'd broken her wrist, no matter that I did barely anything but prepare her little mouse meals, button her housedresses, and sweep now and then. Since there was little to do in Ely that time of year besides visit the library— or, as Julia suggested, "Go stand in the wind and get the stink blown off you"—I got a mountain of reading done, the month more like a long visit than caretaking.

From the maternal side of the family, I inherited Grandmother Emily's wicker table and chair. The wicker is bonded with decades of paint—a chip revealing at least six colors, currently a glossy gray green—and waiting for the next porch it will live in should there ever be one.

And things of Dad's. Not much—mostly books, a few bits of furniture, his tape measure, and one of those folding padded seats to cushion his skinny butt from the aluminum bench of his fishing boat. Just stuff I've hung onto, stuff he probably bought at Salvation Army.

Seven

Sometimes the draw feels like the tug of a compass needle, an unseen force. Maybe the north is imprinted genetically, or perhaps it's been one of the few constants in life. Friends, lovers, relatives weave in and out, come and go, die. Marriages fail, life tumbles, a promising career arches, then plummets. My son grows up, leaves home, leaves the *country*. Interests wane, directions shift. One thing doesn't change; it just hunkers a couple hundred miles away. Whether life is being gently rocked or swamped, the land is just *there*.

Having been in and out of thrall with the north so long, I still don't know when it began, but I can think of one moment when I was too young to be able to describe it with words, being only seven or eight and not owning the vocabulary. I was barefoot and tripping from the cabin to the shore. Mist still skirted the surface of the lake, and I registered that the mist made a corresponding line to the dew, dragging the hem of my nightie. The wet grass felt oddly distinct underfoot, and I imagined each blade of it, the textures of shiny side/dull side. I could smell it and knew what it would taste like. I was all in chlorophylly tune with the grass, imagining the woof and warp of roots even as my own toes were digging in. Some other eye in my brain opened to map how the roots dipped into the soil for nourishment, weaving turf below while blades above pulled light from the sun to make itself grow, to be, to make itself *grass.*

In this oddly comforting moment came the realization that I could feel safe outside the tight spaces of childhood, that I could belong in the world beyond my current situation, which could be a frightening one. The natural world at last made sense. It was all utterly connected, one thing essential to the other. The trees needed the water needed the air needed the wind needed the sun, and the clouds needed all and vice versa and so on. *All* somehow pitched in with time to make *now,* and I knew even with my dearth of words that I was most alive at that moment and that one either is or isn't. The piece of driftwood knocking itself in the surf wasn't. The living tree next to me was. *I* was.

For a long time, I connected that moment of buoyancy as being specific to the north, though I know now it can happen anywhere because it has: on a rainy street of yellow taxis reflecting their drunken twins over wet pavement, once during a frost while walking furrows in a southern field, and again staring out an airplane at the glow of a city a mile below. Mostly the clarity visits when alone, when the mind is so empty it drops its tether to consciousness, which springs up to bite the present.

I curse such instances and am grateful for them. Did one dewy morning when I was momentarily possessed by my surroundings land me back here?

Places look better from far away. Except they aren't, and I'm not the only person drawn by the perceived romance of this place, taken in by it, thrilled by it, disillusioned by it, or even spat out by it. It's tough here.

It's not for everyone, but every year a few hundred thousand canoeists from across the planet apply a year in advance for a BWCAW permit and the chance to cast themselves into a true wilderness. They arrive having dreamt of the trip, planned, and anticipated. Maybe they've subscribed to *Outside*, read the Sigurd Olson books, mooned over the Brandenburg photographs. They've shopped REI or Patagonia for clothing made of engineered feather-light fabrics that if sold by weight would cost seven hundred dollars a pound. Their canoes are translucent Kevlar or cedar strip with custom paddles. The cameras are high-def digital SLRs with waterproof sleeves. They hope the trip will be soul-crackingly beautiful, that they will be one with nature.

Then there are the seasoned regulars who put in with their aluminum canoes and slapdash gear, less intent on the paddling and scenery than on getting to their favorite fishing holes. They're going to land a lunker and get some fresh air. The pretty vistas are a nice bonus.

Several friends are frequent visitors to the Boundary Waters. When given a second glass of something, they often relay accounts that exaggerate the bests and the worsts of a trip. As they tell it (roughly), a typical day begins at dawn, when: You start by wriggling from the cocoon of a sleeping bag that is separated from the hardest stone on earth by a half-inch sleeping pad. First order of the day is beating your limbs to get blood circulating. The sudden exposure to cold air prompts the next immediacy— to pee. Puppet-leg it into the boreal dim to the camp pit toilet and bare your nether bits in the same brush where carnivorous mammals are eager for their own breakfasts, where deer ticks are cocked and aimed.

That chanced and accomplished, you must build a fire so that vacuum-packed shards of food can be reconstituted with water that hopefully has had the parasitic Giardia boiled or filtered out of it. Coffee is essential, so much so that you may have scrimped on a few other essentials while packing, like extra socks and batteries, in favor of the 2.5-pound Tomiko K2 espresso kit.

Perched on a picturesque rock in morning light, you might enjoy an espresso better than any from the cafés of Montmartre or Florence. It hardly matters that the creamer is a powdered by-product or that the cup is lip-scorching aluminum alloy; you very well might, in the lull before the insects *du jour* converge, experience a true coffee moment. A fellow camper might capture such a moment in a photograph of the sort seen on glossy ads for anything from the aforementioned Tomiko K2 espresso maker to emergency bee sting kits or quick-dry underpants. Such satisfying moments invariably lead to other less romantic post-coffee moments that involve trekking back to the latrine with scant squares of toilet paper, muttering a prayer for brevity.

After calamine lotion is applied and ticks tweezed and DEET sprayed, every item in camp is tediously repacked and loaded into canoes, and the adventure begins. The paddle in your yet-unblistered hand feels light. You set off under either a soft sun with calm waters or a punishing sun, or eerie fog, or rain, or a wind that either blasts, gusts, or blows from whatever direction makes it a headwind. Snow in May is more common than you might think. This is real paddling, and it will be the reason that by end of day your shoulders and forearms will howl. The first day may be easy with a single portage, during which you pry provisions and packs from canoes and haul them overland from one put-in to another before trudging back for more. When strapping on the pack over sunburnt shoulders, you might experience some regret over the espresso maker and its carrying case; surely the 1.5-pound model would have sufficed.

Portages are serenaded by buzzing, slaps, grunts, obscenities, and sighs—part and parcel of a canoe trip trudging alongside in fellowship with someone who would paddle-throttle you if they suspected you were hoarding a Mars bar. By nightfall, should it ever come, you're thrilled to eat a half-cooked, unidentifiable meal charred over butane. Then you pitch sideways onto a ledge of Canadian Shield, too tired to wish for an OxyContin. After five or six such days, campers emerge with stories to tell, women often using childbirth analogies, the only other experience to rival such exquisite misery. But memories warp in the backward lens of time and one *forgets,* going on to birth more babies or make return visits to the Boundary Waters during the heat of July or the snows of June. If an episiotomy requiring twenty-six stitches can be forgotten, so too might a 260-rod portage in a downpour. Highlights and details of canoe trips often grow more florid with each telling. The actual steepness of rapids grows steeper, the lengths of portages grow longer, a fondly recalled sunset glows every bit as fiery and colorful as the pass of an obstetric scalpel.

Amnesia aside, when packing for the next trip you might let practicality prevail and leave the espresso kit behind, knowing full well that next time you'd be thrilled with freeze-dried Folgers or a steaming cup of spit if it contained caffeine.

We embrace the adventure, the romance; admire the beauty of the wilderness, hoping to experience the experience. But shouldn't we also be wary, even *afraid?* Occasional stories I hear remind me we are not in charge.

A seasoned guide told me about being approached by a very young wayward cougar. Knowing that where there is cougar off-spring, an anxious cougar mother is not far behind, she quickly stepped in front of one of her group, blocking a woman from Ohio who was *reaching* for the cute thing. Just then, the momma came roaring into their midst, and the campers went more or less paralytic. Amazed, they watched as the mother simply snatched up her kitten by the scruff and leapt away. The guide did what I would have—wet her pants. In fact, she said, there wasn't a dry pair on the trail.

At the laundromat, a very tan girl cramming her stinky clothes into the washer next to mine grew slowly more talkative, as if getting used to her voice again, reporting she'd just had the most amazing shower ever, using soap for the first time in weeks. Her damp hair was plastered to her arms, which I couldn't help notice were bruised and hatched with scratches. She traced one, saying, "Yeah, you think you know someone . . . ," then pro-ceeded to tell the story of how she and her best friend from col-lege embarked on a two-week canoe trip, only to discover by day three that they despised each other. But in true passive-aggressive Minnesota fashion, they just carried on, barely speaking. By day eleven, they finally had it out. The girl laughed as she described how they had rolled around "on the ground like trailer trash, mud wrestling—except this was real mud with sticks and *rocks* in it." She showed off a nasty bruise on her thigh.

When our clothes were dry and we were folding, she mused, "Next time we're gonna go further, into Quetico."

"We?" I asked. "Not the same friend?"

She shrugged. "Well, at least we'll know what we're in for."

Across from the laundromat is an Internet café, one of the few places in town where locals mingle with summer people, which include campers, canoeists, resort guests, and cabin owners. In the café, I keep both ears cocked, sometimes pretending to be writing a list, which I sometimes am, of people's words. Folks talk, and if I'm feeling bold, I might lean in with "I couldn't help but hear you say . . ." and am sometimes rewarded with the sort of story you hear over the breakfast counter, the bar, or tanks at the bait shop—abrupt stories that get told northern style, with few adjectives.

A man named Hurly considered his unlit Marlboro in the Portage Bar, telling me he'd been meaning to quit since he promised the Good Lord he would while fighting whitecaps and high winds on the Canadian side of Basswood Lake. "Yup, I says to Him, if I make landfall, that's it, not another cancer stick ever."

Hurly didn't look like he could even get into a canoe, so I asked when that was.

"Thirty-seven years now," he coughed, "give or take a few months."

At the outfitters where we sometimes shower, a woman with an Ace bandage on her ankle was rinsing off her grossly caked Tevas. She'd been portaging with a too-heavy pack, barely able to manage it, when her foot skidded off the path into the maggoty carcass of a deer, trailside kill. She "should have known something was rotten in Denmark" but assumed the stink was coming from just ahead, her husband, who'd been emitting noxious gas from all the freeze-dried food.

When I first told Sam he was going to camp, he asked, "Wha'd I do?"

Of course it was fine once he got there. He had fun and went on to attend summer camp, canoe camp, fly-fishing camp, and winter camp at places with many-syllabled names like Widjiwagan and Icaghowan. He can handle a canoe or kayak, can pitch a tent, and has the basics of camping down. Still, he has yet to feel entirely comfortable in nature and may never acclimate to the outhouse and the wolf spiders that occasionally chase him out, his pants not quite up and showing a winking of white bum as he bolts, shrieking a little.

There are those who come to the Boundary Waters for outdoor adventure, beauty, and solitude, but the area has long attracted other types as well. Perhaps because of the remoteness, there's always been a fringe population here. Early on it was socialists and immigrants seeking asylum and work, grandparents and great-grandparents of locals. More recent newcomers include loners and eccentrics, dropouts from the big cities, back-to-the-landers, fairy campers, homeschoolers, devil worshippers, fundamentalists, survivalists, cranks, stoners, artists, *writers.*

My own identity here often feels murky and undefined; I have a local name and history, but I'm a 612er, a poseur in a flannel shirt with suspicious motives, scrutinizing the place through voyeur's goggles. There's no real glue to hold me here with my family gone, and my effort to wedge in sometimes feels futile and even silly, as if my presence puts a finger in the dam of time that

I might reclaim some lost connection in hopes my son and I will be happy here and feel at home, *have* a home. Will embracing this place provide some firm ground from which to launch our futures—will it embrace *us?* Maybe yes, maybe no. It's too soon to tell.

Eight

When two major mining test sites were blasted on the northernmost boundary of the land, one was called East Lumbering Bear, the other West Lumbering Bear. Why, I wondered? On a map, you might interpret our lake as being partially shaped like a lumbering bear but only if you squint or are drunk. Maybe a bear lumbered through on the day the place was named? Our lake has had more than one name; some maps say one thing, another claims it's something else altogether.

There's lots of waffling around here when it comes to names and mottos, one morphing into another every dozen or so years as if trying to get it right.

Charles Kuralt dubbed the area "End of the Road" after buying the local radio station. His catch phrase has stuck with those nostalgic for Ely's brush with celebrity, though it pretty much *was* the end of the road for Kuralt, who died soon afterward. To me the motto has an admittedly not-so-positive ring, like "bought the farm."

I like "The Land of Sky-Blue Waters" best. It's descriptive and suggests a cartoon bear might come by to hand you a cold one. I vaguely remembered Hamm's ads of the sixties portraying an iconic version of the north. When I logged onto YouTube to watch a few of the commercials, I was surprised at just how un-PC they were, with tom-tom beats and cartoon rain dances and grinning "Injuns," but others were alluring for their idyllic take on our wilderness, probably doing as much to promote tourism as alcohol consumption. The hook was that the water Hamm's was brewed with was the freshest and coldest!—the message being "this is some clean beer." The subliminal suggestion was that northern Minnesota is one big campground where all trees are pine, and life is a very long fishing trip. My local liquor store still stocks Hamm's, though it's now brewed in another state, and I don't imagine it tastes any better than it did (like pee, Dad claimed), and the ceaselessly cascading waterfall of the electric Hamm's bar sign only fools me into thinking *I* have to pee.

There's also "God's Country," which works if you're keen to dismiss millions of years of geology, biology, and evolution. Call me a killjoy for the Almighty, but I'm a killjoy with two feet planted on terra firma that has folded up and folded again and heated and cooled to show off the groovy banded red Jasper underfoot, evidence of just how the place was actually formed. If you insist on throwing some god into the equation, why not call it "Vulcan's Country"? I try to understand the creationist's perspective, but when I look around at what nature has wrought, that thinking seems medieval. Even in face of irrefutable science, I feel woefully outnumbered by those who are certain that after death they are bound for heaven—a better version of here with fewer mosquitoes—or hell—a much shittier version where every month is February.

"Gateway to the Wilderness" is the literal brand, as evocative as any chosen by committee, reminding me of the Minneapolis motto in the eighties that insisted, rather defensively, "We Like It Here!" (even if you don't!). "Mesabi" is what the Ojibwe call the region, anthropomorphizing the place in numerous but similar ways. I gave up after five translations. "The Giant's Place," "The Grandmammy of All Places," "The Sleeping Giant," "The Sleeping Grandmother," "Big Grandmother" all convey about the same message: be warned, pioneer—think twice before trying to breach this dame's backyard.

"Incredibly Rocky Place" is one name you don't hear, yet it's hands down the most descriptive. Rock is the defining characteristic; there's more of it than water or trees. This land is nothing if not geological. The only stonier place I've seen lies off the Irish coast, where the Aran Islands hump upward in postcard images of cobblestone lanes and stone fences encasing rocky pastures and stone cottages. Most of the soil on Aran is actually man-made, a mixture of composted seaweed and fish offal, sand, manure, and human urine to break it all down. The rest was hauled over rough seas from the mainland in little skin boats called curraghs. Just as stony is the famous Burren over on the mainland, a place Oliver Cromwell and his men considered an inhospitable nuisance in their crusade, calling the Burren "a savage land, yielding neither water enough to drown a man, nor tree to hang him, nor soil enough to bury him." You'd think stoning might have occurred to them, or maybe just dashing the heretics and monks to the ground.

The first of our own numerous confrontations with rock came when considering an outhouse. Hindsight is a wise teacher, as are the mistakes of others. The traditional two-seater at our old family cabin was down a path that seemed long but was in reality only about thirty feet from the cabin, probably not far enough in the eyes of the county inspector. A journey to the outhouse at night was best embarked on with some bravado and a sister. It helped if Dad stood outside the cabin watching until we reached the door so Sasquatch couldn't pluck us from the path. A sprint and door slam and we were inside, where flashlights cast shadows where there were normally none. Above the bench was a sign: *This is a High Class Place, Act Respectable.* The only other adornment was a painting predating the black velvet tourist variety: a cockatiel on his perch with real, actual feathers glued to it. Since there was so little to look at in the outhouse, every detail of that bird picture is etched to memory, down to the carved scallops of the frame, which at some point got painted the same mint sherbet color as the walls. The outhouse always had dated copies of *Time, Newsweek,* or *Reader's Digest,* but we weren't about to be there long enough to read anything at night, not even cartoons. An upside-down Maxwell House can protected the toilet paper from rodents, and if ever someone forgot to cover the roll, the next morning the outhouse floor would be festive as a snow globe. We had to wonder, did the mice and voles really patrol every night in the hopes some stupid human had forgotten the whole coffee can routine?

I have a frame-worthy photo of the outhouse in its last stand, crowded by spruce, a closet-sized building painted a color not found in nature, a clownish aqua clashing with its roof of olivey, bumpy moss. It leans, not a little.

The practicality of a two-seater outhouse still eludes me even after old-timers have explained the concept—that you sit on one side until the thing is full, then you sit on the other side. Mix it up! Since the seats are all of a foot away from each other, I find this doubtable and suspect there were more people into companion toileting than I care to imagine, though at eight years old I was thrilled to have a pee buddy. The tired joke then was about a two-story outhouse with one hole upstairs and another on the main floor belonging to the fill-in-the-blank-with-an-ethnic-slur neighbors. In these parts, those would have included Polack, Bohunk, Wop, Canuck, Kraut, and Swede, which either didn't warrant a slur or was considered one on its own. In all its years of use, our old outhouse was moved onto a newly dug pit only once. Where did all that going go?

The new outhouse was being built at Lars's sawmill. It was a thing to behold and built like Fort Knox, as if to protect its contents from being stolen. Inside, the seat was so high it required a step, like a real throne. Still undetermined was what would happen *underneath* it. Options to consider included a hand-turned compost chamber with active and inactive compartments, which works by letting waste accumulate for a week or so, adding with each go just the right amount of untreated sawdust of just the right texture and dryness (acquired from a lumberyard). After a week, you open the door to both compartments from the outside and shovel the contents from the active side to the inactive, "curing" side. This is the most environmentally sound and grossest option, and one I've had firsthand experience with. As one of ten or so women in a retreat group for over a period of eight years, I spent time on Mallard Island in Rainy Lake, the former home of conservationist Ernest Oberholtzer and now a foundation hosting creative and environmental groups. Near the end of our stay, we drew straws, and us losers donned our grungiest camp clothes and tied perfumed bandanas across our faces, reasoning that we might as well gag on Jovan Musk than our own efforts. We grabbed shovels, breathed through our mouths, and just did it. On a Bad Toilet Day, the problem was usually liquid in nature so that on the ensuing Bad Poetry Night there would be lines inspired by the moments of our chore as sublime as "turds forlorn and floating corn."

Building a composting chamber on our site would require a cement mixer and running water, which we did not have. Plus the outhouse would have to be built atop the chamber, which likely wouldn't be sturdy enough for the behemoth that was taking shape. So manual composting was a no-go. An electric composter would have been ideal, but there wasn't solar power yet, and even if there were, it wouldn't be reliable or constant enough.

A few outhouses around the lake employ a chemical liquid method with plastic barrels sunk as deep as possible into the ground, topped with an elevated structure, the end result much like a taller, more attractive porta-potty. After a season, the local honey wagon—in this case, Royal Flush—comes and pumps out the barrels, same as pumping a septic system. In theory this is the best option, but to get anywhere near these toilets is to realize either the chemical ratio or the ventilation isn't right because rather than masking the odor of waste, it's somehow enhanced, an acrid stench that makes hand-turned composting a bed of roses in comparison.

With some hired help, Lars dug the hole, but just when they hit bedrock, his back gave out. He could have called in Boulder Busters, the local rock eradication service, but that might have seemed akin to giving in. I couldn't help but think a dynamite charge like those used to blast Lumbering Bear might be the ticket. The hole didn't look like it was going to get any deeper, and Lars went in for back surgery.

Apparently we'd have the standard, old-fashioned outhouse I grew up with—a hole in the ground with a building squatting over it. Once planted, the outhouse wouldn't be going anywhere; there would be no second hole. I could only hope that the shallow dent would suffice until we had an indoor bathroom, when the outhouse could become optional, or a shed, since we still didn't have one.

A conventional outhouse is actually fairly environmentally sound and doesn't stink when treated properly. A percentage of the waste seeps away, and the rest breaks down with the aid of time and lime (calcium oxide). Lime is nasty stuff. When Henry III was defending English shores, his army defeated the marauding French by hurling lime into their eyes and blinding them. In the battle on stink, lime is sprinkled down the outhouse hole after one's efforts. Though it's a natural substance, lime, if inhaled, can scar or destroy a septum as efficiently as a hill of cocaine. It can also sear skin, and applying water or ice only raises its temp to 150 degrees. This is one of the few instances where leaving the toilet seat *down* is the offense; any lime left on a seat can blister a painful ring on delicate flesh. If only "flush" were an option.

A girl can dream.

Nine

"Stonich is an Ely name. You otta put a sign out there at your driveway: that way your place won't get vandalized."

"Even the meth heads know enough to not trash a local's cabin."

"Sometimes you gotta do a little name dropping."

"Even if it's just your own."

This sound advice comes from two fellows in Dee's Lounge on Ely's main street. One had been in the mines with my Uncle Ted. They told me that if I was just asking questions, their names were Juri and Earl, but if I was planning on writing anything that their wives might read, revealing they'd been in Dee's all afternoon with some female, then they were Mutt and Jeff. They howled over their joke and took it further by correcting anyone who came in and addressed one of them, "He mighta been Juri this morning, but he's Mutt now!" Earl (Jeff) slapped his knee.

Though I was over forty, I was still introduced as "the Stonich girl that made up that book about here."

There was a lot of subdued chatter in the bar. Just out was the news that a bunch of young local men and a juvenile had been arrested for accosting a group of campers within the Boundary Waters, threatening them both verbally and with weapons. Shots had been fired. Both Juri and Earl knew most of the boys charged. Both used "we" and "us" when talking about their community. Most everyone in Dee's knew at least one of the accused.

Juri smacked the bar. "Tourists're gonna think we're a bunch of backwater hicks, like in that movie . . ."

"*Deliverance,*" Earl finished for him. "These boys are all charged with terroristic threats."

"More like *asshole-istic,* if you ask me. 'Terroristic' makes us sound like a bunch of towelheads."

"Right, but whatever you call what they did, it leaves us twisting in the wind to make things right." Earl swept an arm to indicate everyone in the bar.

"Like we got time to be goodwill ambassadors on top of everything else."

"They shouldn't 'a been in there with motorboats anyway."

"Well, that's another issue altogether."

Attitudes here are as mild as the weather. Most residents have wildly differing opinions on issues from declassifying wolves off the endangered species list to potential copper mining or the use of motorized vehicles in restricted areas. Political arguments are heated. Moral attitudes are more private, though often evidenced in the plastering of bumper stickers, some indicating that the drivers are both pro-life *and* pro-war, or letting us know what their personal Jesus would Do, Say, Buy, or Bomb. My favorite sticker says as much about the place as the people, applied to the back of a rusted Land Rover: SHIT HAPPENS.

Ely made national news when its city council officially denounced the invasion of Iraq, then made the news again the following week when they revoked that denunciation after a vivid dispute between council members who were split on the issue, members of the antiwar coalition, the then mayor, and veterans who interpreted the vote as anti-troop and anti-American. There is little neutral ground here—radios are tuned to public radio, AM conservative talk shows, or eighties rock.

If isolation fosters extremism, northern Minnesota is a potential incubator for nutcases on either end. A fanatic, as my father defined one, is anybody with his head so far up his own ass he can't smell anyone else's. I guessed that meant a zealot was somebody who feared and distrusted anyone who didn't understand or smell the world in the same way he did. On the road north, you're welcomed to the region by an array of signs planted next to Highway 53 near Cotton, where for decades a landowner has been posting hand-painted billboards that change as his beefs do. Sometimes the signs are illustrated with primitive drawings, as if painted by a sort of Curmudgeon Moses. At the height of the anti-French sentiment that swept Real America a number of years ago, the curmudgeon painted the UN flag being urinated on by a poodle, with the words "Piss on the Poodles, and Kofi Annan too!" Curmudgeon also seems to harbor great disdain for the Postmaster General and pretty much whoever is in power. His most recent billboard rant depicts President Obama as a half-naked spearchucker with a wide grin. I want badly to interview this man, but the fact that his compound is surrounded by ten-foot fencing made of scrap metal with a sign that warns "No Trespassing, Injury Very Likely" would dissuade most anyone from approaching his bunker, or spaceship-in-progress, or whatever it is he lives in behind the scary fence.

When I Googled an Ely topic, the first hit was an article published in a small Punjabi newspaper written by an Indian reporter. Ely might seem an odd place for the World Press Institute to send its fellows, but it's done just that for years, hosting an annual gathering of international journalists, with locals opening their homes to the visiting foreigners. At the latest forum, when the issue of gun control arose, most of the journalists offered that in their own countries, guns are highly restricted. Then the mayor weighed in that in Ely there is this saying: "My wife, yes; my dog, maybe; my gun, *never.*" This is the sort of *Deliverance* response that Earl and Juri cringe over, knowing it will only color perceptions of the place. They are trying to earn a living and well understand that tourism depends on outsiders. More recently, the same mayor was charged with theft and illegally entering the BWCA, an offense he's been cited for numerous times since 1978, despite federal regulations that designate it as wilderness.

"Which, *hello,* is exactly what brings tourists and their money here." Juri rolls his eyes.

Earl insists folks here do read more than just the local paper, most are law-abiding and can properly interpret the Constitution, and they *do* welcome diversity and more awareness of the world beyond. Of course, as in any small town, there are also those who want nothing of the world, and Earl says it's sometimes hard to tell one from another. It's senseless to judge an old-timer holding up the bar at Zaverl's when he says things like "That Negro fella is doing a pretty good job so far" because it's possible the geezer was out hunting during the decades of political correctness and missed the phases of rephrasing and probably thinks GLBT is some new sandwich down at the café. A few are intentionally up front in their prejudices, like the Foghorn Leghorn store clerk from the South who crows his own brand of intolerance within earshot of anyone buying a bag of finishing nails, claiming he isn't afraid to call a spade a spade and that one of the reasons he moved this far north was "'cause they ain't none."

Historically the Range has remained a predominantly Democratic, pro-union, and labor stronghold, but most people keep views to themselves or limit them to their fishing buddies or coffee klatches, aware that this is indeed a small place and that we do all have to live together. One thing everyone agrees on is that Ely is an interesting place, not an easy place, to live. City limits are only a concept here, and the community nets out to include anybody for whom Ely is the hub. We're all neighbors, whether separated by blocks or miles, rivers or bays. "Town" is where we go to get groceries, check e-mail, trawl the farmer's market, do laundry, get food we can't have at The Lake like pizza or ice cream, or just hang around the coffee shop and listen to voices that aren't radio. Ely is much changed since my childhood in the sixties, when I cannot recall there being a stoplight.

My grandmother Julia died in 1987, just when change for the better was finally coming after years of the Iron Range holding itself close against a long recession, mine closures, and flagging tourism. She would be impressed to see the town now, thriving as a vacation destination, though she might shake her head at the touristy "shoppes." She would have laughed off the concept of *new* furniture for a cabin or special clothes for fishing.

It would have pleased my father that fifty thousand additional acres were added to the protected BWCA after his death, that the place remains pristine and has been kept from the fate of other vacation regions across the state, where shores are pocked with over-development as if Woodbury or Eagan had been dragged north and dropped lakeside.

Dad had a particular gripe over use and abuse of snowmobiles and ATVs. When the first three-wheelers were just appearing in the mid-seventies, he derisively called them "trikes," shaking his head and exclaiming, "Grown men driving them!"

We are the lucky few to be near places of true wilderness, where the land is preserved in a triumvirate of amazing parks: the Boundary Waters, Quetico, and Voyageurs. It's easy to take for granted that such places are here for us, but their preservation didn't come easily, and the battle to save this jewel box of wilderness was long and fraught. Many are familiar with the writings and voice of Sigurd Olson, but only some know the work of conservationists like Ernest Oberholtzer, who lobbied and toiled tirelessly in spite of financial hardship and even personal threats. Dozens of people worked for decades to stave off industry, to warn the government of the bleakness of a future without wilderness, and to educate the citizens. Individuals behind the various battles included some familiar names, like Frank Hubachek of the Wilderness Research Center, Bob Marshall of the Forest Service, Aldo Leopold (*before* he was Aldo Leopold), Robert Sterling Yard, Benton MacKaye, Harvey Broome, Bernard Frank, Harold Anderson, and others. Presidential examples set by both Roosevelts encouraged such men to fight when opposed by the until then omnipotent industrialists. Preserving wilderness might be one of FDR's greatest achievements along with his job programs like the WPA and the Civilian Conservation Corps, both directly benefiting our park systems. Perhaps the most important message the conservationists finally got across to the American people was that wild places are *necessary*. If they didn't exist, how could we possibly know now what the untouched, unsullied wild actually looks like, feels like, smells like? To lose it would be to lose *natural* history. Maybe equally important is the growing relevance of gauging our own impacts on the planet by comparing them to these rare unimpacted environments.

Here, most of the drama is external. The glaciers that raked and carved the land made it both beautiful and difficult. Life *is* harder here, and the hardship is often credited as building character. Maybe it bulks up a certain tenacity, but it sometimes seems life here can constrict character—the isolation, the months of workdays begun and ended in darkness, with no time for leisurely chat outdoors because your nose hairs are iced, your face is numb, and your dog will freeze to the sidewalk if you don't keep pace. There is a taciturnity that prevails here. People are not terribly outgoing, but they are far from unkind. They are not always talkative, but they do have stories. Some can be suspicious of outsiders, or just tolerant. This isn't the South; stories are told quickly with little embellishment. Time matters: sunlight is limited, and there's wood to chop, diesel to pump, sidewalks to clear, hotdish to bake, batteries to jump. Life is short.

Ten

Since I was building here, was going to *be* here, shouldn't I be interacting more with the locals, be less an observer, more of a citizen? Maybe have some fun, get to know somebody—perhaps even Biblically. It had been a long time since I'd dated, but the idea grew on me once I looked around and realized there were plenty of outdoorsy, handsome guys on the streets of Ely.

Alas, there are woefully few venues for singles to meet besides the VFW and the few local bars like Dee's Polka Lounge, the Portage, Zaverl's, and establishments I'd never gotten around to, like the Kwazy Wabbit, with its sign hung upside down. In Dee's I met an interesting man I would have considered desirable if he hadn't stood up to become less so by not being able to stay upright unaided. Less shit-faced was what I was hoping for.

In such a small town, the question then was, if not the bars, *where?* I could hang out around portages and put-ins as if just passing by, or frequent the building supply yard, the union hall, or canoe outfitters, trying to look nonchalant ("Have we met?") Or I could crash a booya dinner at the Jugoslav Hall where I might nab a hottie with his own rolling oxygen. The odds of getting a decent date on this side of the Laurentian Divide were as good as winning Powerball but not as good as being struck by lightning.

While parked to check my cell messages at the one high spot in town, I had a view of a full parking lot and a quiet revelation. Maybe the best read one could get on local bachelors is by simply checking out their vehicles. You are what you drive here. What a man's truck says about him is as telling as having brunch with his mother: size of gun rack, number of axles, types of load racks and hitches (does he pull an ATV trailer or haul canoes?). What's in the truck bed? Too clean? Too dirty? Is the radio tuned to AM? What sort of discarded food containers and wrappings litter his dash? Who's his bobblehead? What's hanging from his rearview mirror? Is that a teeny *propeller* adorning his trailer hitch? Bumper stickers and magnetic ribbons are almost too easy. Little window decals reveal affiliations to AAA, AARP, DFL, GOP, IBEW, NRA, NPR, PETA, or UMWA. What, or whom, is the little Calvin decal peeing on? License plates offer evidence of whether the driver's a veteran, a volunteer fireman, or just dweeb enough to have vanity plates. Damage to the rear bumper? Passive. Dents to the sides? Distracted. Front bumper? Aggressive!

During a rainy family reunion, my sisters and I sat in a cabin on Jasper Lake discussing man-catching strategies. I told them my idea for stalking parking lots, which they agreed was a good idea in theory, but a) Who has time?, b) Just how *does* one approach some guy in his truck?, and c) How does one determine if said guy is single?

No matter what, I'd seem like a psycho.

Trips to town suggested that the ratio of males to local females was definitely in my favor. All I'd really need to do was tack up a poster next to the lost dog fliers around town: "Female, breathing."

"Maybe a *little* more," suggested Mary, who'd once worked writing ad copy. "You know, 'height/weight proportional,' or perhaps a sort of teaser, like 'must love taxidermy.'"

"Right," Valerie added. "Things *men* like."

"What," I asked, "beer, blowjobs, and *bowling?*"

Julie, not fully in, popped her head up, "You'd go bowling?"

I opted for Internet dating, joining one of the hipper online sites where potential dates looked less desperate. I fiddled with writing a profile and cast around for a photo that was an honest enough likeness yet would make my eyes seem less close together. While I was filling in the blank for age limit of potential dates, Sam looked over my shoulder, asking, "*What* is desirable about fifty-five?"

Note to single mothers: Never ask your teenage son for help with a dating profile. Do not allow him in the same room, and definitely do not ask which photo makes you look datable.

On the other hand, any man I might seriously date would eventually have to pass muster with my child. A newcomer would have to *get* us and would have to accept our many familial quirks, like our habit of speaking in gargled Glaswegian accents *à la Trainspotting*. When we read or told stories, we endeavored to do so in character, shooting for authenticity, and believe me it's not easy to keep cadence through *A Child's Christmas in Wales* maintaining a Welsh brogue. Sam was surrounded all day by people with accents, in his Spanish immersion school and at home with Laura, our Spanish exchange student, and Duffer, the lovely Scot who often worked around the house, watched Sam, and occasionally cooked. Sam still waxes nostalgic for her shepherd's pie, shaking his head over my attempts, asking, "Whay cahn y'nay scrrrape it op lake our Dahfferr?" He'd also seen more than his share of foreign films of all vintages and was perhaps the only teenage boy alive ever to have claimed, "Maggie Smith is *hot.*" Sam became an adroit mimic, though my favorite of his impressions was accent free (*word* free, actually) and of a Minnesotan, consisting of one very exaggerated, seemingly endless, old-mannish, loooong suck-it-in-inhale through the nose: his Garrison Keillor.

Whatever man if any that might step into our fray would have to be a good sport, prepared to leave the hamming to others. He would have to take us part and parcel, a two-for-one deal. And Sam would have to at least *like* him.

The dating site took in my information, personal desires, and credit card details and within a few days spat out a total of *two* not-quite matches within fifty miles of the Ely zip code. The vaguely interesting one was widely read and self-employed but hinted that what he did was nobody's business. He lived off the grid in a sort of enclave described in a way that hinted Una-bomber. The other, a therapist transplanted from out east, said he liked to cook, which I thought was a good sign; cooking could mean he was in touch with his inner domestic. Then his e-mail response came back with a smiley emoticon :-) and additional photos that revealed he not only liked to cook but eat—a lot. He wasn't even close to being HWP though his profile claimed he was. Sure, *once* :-))

At my age, I wasn't up for much compromise and at least knew what I *wasn't* looking for. I updated my search to cast a wider net that included the Twin Cities. Within a day my mailbox filled. It seemed there were lots of matches in the metro area. Then I realized most profiles tended to include a shocking amount of fiction—men portraying themselves not so much as who they are but as whom they would like to see cast as themselves in the film of their dream lives. Over-representing or misrepresenting oneself on a profile seemed so pointless. No matter what the ruse, it was bound to fall flat over the first date.

Bachelor Number One was handsome and interesting, definitely showing promise right up until the bill came. We both had the same meal at dinner, and we each had a beer. When it was time to split the tab, he tallied it to factor the price difference of my bottled beer to his draft beer, making my share seventy-nine cents more. I paid my extra and then covered for his miserly 10 percent tip. Date over.

My second date lasted minutes. Bachelor Number Two somehow knew my identity and had Googled me, even though by then everyone knew it was bad form to *go ogle* somebody before a date. He admitted he wasn't actually interested in dating but *had* brought along a manuscript he'd written, thinking I might like to look it over. I rose to leave abruptly enough to spill coffee, not quite on his lap but at least on his manuscript.

Bachelor Number Drunk looked so unlike his profile photo he might have stolen it. We met for an early weekend brunch, during which he had to get three Bloody Marys down before his hands stopped shaking. Date over just as he was ordering a fourth, implying to the server that I was a party pooper for not joining in.

Others weren't much better, more like skits than dates. One I remember absolutely nothing of except a flash of when the man crossed his legs, revealing that he wore sock garters.

I was disheartened but not surprised to discover how many men over forty were rabidly uninterested in women over forty, one claiming, "I don't do carbon dating." The women's profiles revealed that many of them caved to that mindset, obviously lying about their ages, eager to appear young and hot. Many had telltale boob jobs and brassy foiled hair, and some even posted glamour shots. Of course, they got more responses than those "physically authentic" models like me, but then I wasn't looking for a guy who would date a self-proclaimed Youthful! Sexy! Fox! Internet dating for women my age seemed like some sort of scramble to beat the expiration of a freshness date. If we didn't find someone we'd dry up and die alone like some crazy aunt who sleeps under butcher paper with her ferrets.

All I wanted was a decent guy to hang out with, but it began to look like I'd have to build him myself, like Mary Shelley. After more not-quite compelling dates, I had one that I *thought* went well, which led to a second, wherein my radar missed a few subtle warning signs, which led to an unfortunate but brief bout with a lawyer who, like a bad onion, just kept revealing more layers of rotten and worse, turning out to be an alcoholic con artist using his two adorable little girls as props. By the time I came to my senses—a matter of weeks—he had abandoned his immigrant clients, had been disbarred, and was evicted from his apartment. With that misstep under my belt, I was left doubting my judgment and instincts and waving good-bye to the money I'd stupidly lent him.

Suddenly, just determining someone's intentions seemed like too much bother. Even if I found an honest guy who was smart and funny and cute and didn't have annoying habits like cocaine or Jack Daniel's for breakfast, then there was the next phase, during which what is buried roils the surface—the quirks, dislikes, obsessions, emotional baggage, fart protocol, or that thing he does with his teeth. Surely romance wasn't always this complex, this conditional?

In 1906, my grandmother Julia was a bright eighteen-year-old approaching pretty and destined for the spinster heap, obviously too choosy given the ample opportunities she had while working in the family catering business. She had a front-and-center seat from which to check out the most eligible men at the many weddings she worked, where all the bachelors were looking their best if not their cleanest.

"Get 'em good and drunk" was an early dating tip doled out to my sisters and me. With Julia's vantage point, she'd have been privy to what category of inebriate every bachelor in the region was: volatile, charming, maudlin, clownish, sloppy, harmless, or teetotaler. Such bits of dating wisdom seemed obvious; others were more subtle. One aunt suggested, *"Dance* with them! That way . . ." —she lowered her voice— "you'll get an idea of whether he has any rhythm. *You* know, *that* kind of rhythm." This was in the mid-seventies, and I could hardly bring myself to admit to Auntie that lots of girls determined whether a boy might have any rhythm on the dance floor by getting him into bed *first.*

Mother suggested, "Play a game," something competitive like poker or Monopoly to determine what kind of sport he was, the idea being "If he loses his shit over Candyland or Go Fish, run, don't walk." She also recommended tackling some chore or household project to get a bead on a potential mate's temperament, cooperative abilities, and all-around usefulness. Not her exact words, but the sentiment was that if he missed the nail and nailed his thumb and called the hammer and not you a "goddamnsonofabitch," you're on the right track and might safely advance to the bigger challenges of hanging wallpaper and raising children.

An overlooked bit of wisdom and one that's only recently occurred to me is to get a meter reading on what is the deal with his mother. He might hate her vehemently or merely endure her with mild dread or teeth-gritting tolerance. Maybe he's indifferent, or he might admit she's not so bad. Ideally he has some genuine affection and regard: "Mom? She's great!" At the scary level, he's utterly devoted and won't trim his nose hairs without her go-ahead and stutters when caught in the crosshairs of her gaze.

When I thought about it, dating began to look like too much bother. Being alone in the woods started sounding pretty good.

Lots of people live alone quite happily into their old age, and some even live *very* alone in remote locations, like the Root Beer Lady, Dorothy Molter, who spent fifty-six years by herself on an island in Knife Lake. While I'm not eager to die alone and have my decomposing, vole-chewed corpse pried from a cabin floor, there are alluring aspects of being single—to sleep when tired, eat when hungry (or while in the bath)—but aside from living the physical rhythms of *self*, there's the freedom, too, to hang my paint-by-number art collection, eat garlic pasta, sing, answer to no one, and speak loudly amongst my selves. Nothing says I'd have to dress like a logger or cut my own hair. On the other hand, when Dorothy Molter died, her obituary led with "The Nation's Loneliest Woman."

As I closed down my profile and turned off my laptop, it occurred to me that I'd have plenty of alone time to write my own obituary before someone else could.

Eleven

A s Tower's resident tailor, Joseph Stonich would have outfitted most local grooms and been present at many weddings. Miss Julia Tancig would have attended as well, helping to cater the events. Joe might have tried to catch her narrowed eye with some grin or gesture or by making a show of accepting *hors d'oeuvres* from the tray she proffered in her signature posture. He might have employed some lighthearted boldness to get her attention. She might have given it to him, she might not.

This or some similar scenario is how my grandparents met. Grandpa Joe was born in Ljubljana, Slovenia ("Loo-blee-on-ya," just like it looks), but raised in Austria with his family, where he apprenticed to a master tailor. His father was a portrait painter and had a wine concession near the Vienna Opera House during the middle of Franz Joseph's reign. Family lore has it that my wine-peddling/painter great-grandfather also played tuba in the Emperor's marching band.

When Joe immigrated to Chicago in the mid-1890s, he spent his first years in America working for the House of Kuppenheimer, clothiers to the elite. Life would have been exciting for a bachelor in such a city; the skyline was just taking shape, giving Chicago its nickname "City of Big Shoulders." Tailoring wasn't particularly taxing work, and Joe was handsome enough, even with one minutely lazy eye. He was young and bright, spit-shining his new language while embarking on a new life. He was most certainly impeccably dressed.

How he arrived in Minnesota around 1904 is less certain. In the wake of the labor influx to the Iron Range at the turn of the century came many merchants—the butcher, the baker, the steel-toe boot maker. He may have come at the behest of his brother, Stephen, luring him to the wilds of Minnesota where tailors were scarce. Joe thought he'd give it a go, wearing a green visor by day, Magritte bowler by night. After Vienna and Chicago, northern St. Louis County could only have been a shock. But love conquers some, and whatever magic Julia possessed apparently held Joe in more thrall than cosmopolitan life had. He either adapted to or gave in to his new surroundings and proposed to Julia. I know they wrote each other before marrying because she told me so; it was more convenient than walking or biking or borrowing a horse to travel two miles just to go courting. They married in the autumn of 1906, before early winter made commuting difficult.

As it happened, my grandparents were a copacetic match, each possessing the sense of humor and low expectations necessary to pull off a successful union. Of course, as soon as they were married, Julia, Catholic to the gills, started having babies at a speed as if in a relay race from husband to midwife to husband, finally stopping at ten. The Stonichs were a good family. Apparently Tower had its share of *bad* families, being essentially a frontier town much like those in the Wild West, only with fewer horses and worse weather. Driving through today you're hard-pressed to picture Tower as a rollicking burg with hotels, saloons, poker parlors, boardwalks, and women of the night, but it was. The sawmills were zealously clearing the forests, and iron ore madness was at full throttle. Men had money to spend on drink, prostitutes, and clothes.

I imagine the tailor shop as a slightly smoky, masculine space with the aura of a barber shop, maybe with a spittoon at the door and the tang of sewing machine oil replacing hair tonic. There was a bench outside to watch the action on Tower's main street, where Joe could sit when the weather was fine and do hand stitching. In a reversal of roles, he was the family gossip, Julia always more tight lipped and judicious, often biting back her comments and wit, which Joe warned she might choke on one day if she didn't just spit them out.

Joe was admired for his expertise and eye for a well-turned lapel but liked for his sense of humor, a trait which has trickled down the generations with no sign of abating. From a young age, Sam has provided nearly enough entertainment to offset the cost of his upbringing, which, according the MSN Money's Child-Rearing Calculator, is roughly $225,000, not counting college tuition. He so definitely has Dad's wry sense of humor that I sometimes wonder if he isn't channeling. When I'm missing my father or feeling sad, it's no longer about me, it's for their loss, the jokes Sam and Dad didn't get to tell each other, the witty retorts they missed lobbing.

When Joe ordered gift calendars to give to his customers, Julia balked, insisting they were too risqué. The calendar was a sepia scene featuring a shy beauty wearing the demure fashion of the day: chin-high starched shirtwaist and dark skirt falling to the ankles of her button-hooked boots. She is perched on the knee of a dandy in a straw boater, who holds one hand boldly around her waist. Above the oval border is printed, "Joseph Stonich, Tailor." Curving below in minuscule font, "Pressing done while you wait."

"Clothes make the man," said Mark Twain, who was still around during Joe's time, but I imagine my grandfather preferred the quote in its entirety: "Naked people have little or no influence on society." Over the years, Joe clothed countless naked men in two- and three-piece suits of dark tweeds and gabardines, garments appropriate for church, court, coffin, and anything in between. Two pairs of trousers came standard with a suit to extend its life. With the prospering mines came a new rank of customers: managers, supervisors, and engineers. Joe tailored everything from tuxedos to band uniforms and occasionally altered a wardrobe *gratis* for some unfortunate logger or miner, modifying sleeves or trousers to pocket neatly over stumps.

Customers came from all walks, and with his easy manner, Joe got on well with those who couldn't get on with each other. Tension between American-born miners and immigrants was high. Ultimately there was tension between most miners and all management at the Oliver Mining Company. Reading the history of these times, it's apparent corporate greed is no new phenomenon. In 1916, Iron Range mining receipts grossed the hysterical amount of $90 million while a miner's pay averaged around three dollars a day—not even close to proportionate. Working conditions were grim, with backbreaking ten-hour shifts. Time off the job was no picnic, either, with company housing being sub-sub-standard, overcrowded with horrid sanitation and little

ventilation or adequate heat. Shopping provided no retail therapy since goods and groceries transported from Duluth were sold
at the company store at prices inflated by 50 to 100 percent.

At first Joe was neutral in the midst of fractious populations:
management, American-born miners, immigrant miners, the Finnish socialist union organizers, the pro-union and the anti-union
miners. Oddly enough, even some *miners* were anti-union, and
considered lily-livered and summarily despised. Wobblies moved
in to stir the pot to boiling. The waves of incoming scabs were
protected by ranks of Pinkertons along with armed thugs dep-
utized by the mining companies, comprising a security force that
in 1916 numbered nearly fifteen hundred, three times the current
population of Tower. It wasn't long before Joe's sympathies turned
toward the men who couldn't afford his clothes.

During the first decade of Joe and Julia's marriage, most days
brought news as bad as or worse than the day before. Strikes
ground away at normalcy across the Range, and morale frayed.
There was a world war on the horizon. Forest and brush fires
roared in the wake of the lazy logging practices, leaving entire
towns burnt. Feuds were common; crime was rife.

On any given day, my grandfather might have walked through
the thick of the labor conflict, twining through picket lines, cross-
ing barricades on both sides of a parade or protest or squabble
or picnic. And while he couldn't know what was in the hearts
and minds of these men, he did know one thing for certain: who
dressed their tackle to the right and who to the left.

By their tenth anniversary, my grandparents had WWI under
their belts, had produced half a dozen children, had served a
community often in tumult, and had survived a pandemic. That

accomplished, they then took on even more children and the Great Depression.

My aunts recalled their childhoods not as the chaos one might imagine in a family of twelve but as simple, sunny years, chalking up the peace to the fact that their parents were fair, good-humored people and that Julia was a better-than-average cook. As for the rare disharmonies between my grandparents, there are two family stories. One regarded the 1918 influenza outbreak, when Joe did something few immigrants did at that time—took a trip back to Europe, ostensibly on a buying tour for Italian woolens, though my grandmother claimed it a lark. When the time came to leave, two of the children were ill, but Joe went anyway. My father and Julia told their very different versions of this story over coffee and strudel at the kitchen table. Dad, who would have been only eight in 1918, piped up in Joe's defense, frowning. "We weren't *that* sick." To which Grandma replied in her croaky snort, "Jesus wept. *You* weren't sick at all!"

The other story was that Joe came home one day with the deed to an island, having bought it on the sly.

But really, how bad could a guy who sewed his bride's wedding dress be?

The family weathered the Depression by being clever. They made do. Meals were stretched, added to. Things were reused, jerry-rigged, repaired, passed around, shared. Clothes were made, then remade. The Stonichs of Tower probably made it look fairly easy—a handsome, bright gaggle, as poor as everyone else but awfully well turned out. Under my grandparents' tutelage, all the girls learned to sew and tailor. "You can be wearing a burlap dress if it's well cut," Grandpa would say. Grandma gave essentially the same advice about coats, "because in a good coat, you can walk through any door."

That fashion acumen apparently did not filter down to my generation. At lunch one day with my sisters, our Aunt Margaret took one look around the table and declared that the lot of us could rob a bank and never be identified, our clothing was that nondescript.

Even after retiring, Joe continued to sew clothes for his grandchildren, and somewhere exists a photo of my oldest brother as a toddler in the 1940s wearing the requisite plaid hat with flaps, standing like a starfish in his new quilted and belted snowsuit from the House of Joe.

When WWII came, four of the ten Stonich offspring were deployed in Europe and the Pacific, including our Aunt Mary, who was an army nurse-anesthetist in field hospitals and M.A.S.H. units, first in France and ultimately at a surgical unit in Germany, where her patients included both Jews liberated from the camps *and* their former captors, German POWs held in U.S. military custody.

Before the war, my aunts enrolled in Ely Junior College (now Vermilion Community College), earning their tuition working as maids or waitresses in the resorts. They were usually required to board for the summers, meals and bed provided. Helen and Dorothy worked one summer at an upscale lodge that is still in operation and on the National Register of Historic Places or, as Dad would say, famous for having never burnt down. While dining at the lakeside restaurant of that resort a few years ago, Aunt Helen, a very put-together and genteel lady nearing ninety, looked around the picturesque dining room, reminiscing a little regretfully and offering in a whisper, "We were worked awfully hard here, and the owners weren't very kind to the girls." After just one season, they moved on. Helen fondly recalled another resort, Pearson's, where they ate meals with the Pearson family and were treated like kin. The boys worked, too, my father as guide for an outfitter, and at the peak of Prohibition, he delivered liquor by boat to resorts on Lake Vermilion. He called it "hooch" and did outrageous impressions of the old drunk who worked the still. By then, Grandpa Joe was growing his own grapes, sending his younger children out to harvest chokecherries and Juneberries. As the son of a European wine vendor, Joe likely couldn't fathom Prohibition, and Julia claimed that during the Noble Experiment, Joe had concocted quite a few less-than-noble experiments of his own, blueberry being the worst, though she admitted some of his more vinegary vintages made decent enough salad dressings.

My grandparents' marriage played itself out during riveting times. They witnessed one advance and invention after another, from automobiles and safety razors to the Pill, DNA fingerprinting, digital media, and the Internet. "When sheets were white" was my grandmother's reference to any era pre-Eisenhower. And when sheets were white, Tower would have been a constrictive, humdrum sort of place, its very size determining the shape and limits of life. Everyone knew everyone else, and everybody's business was broadcast. Village society must have sometimes felt like a huge dysfunctional family, though in some ways I think, how ideal, to have only your own tribe to worry over and care for when the world beyond town is only a distant concept rather than the bloated, too-busy, hyper-connected place it often seems today.

In the forties, my grandparents moved from their neat, two-story white house in Tower to a neat, two-story house in Ely. Their children fanned out to where jobs and wars took them, many going far. Only one returned to live, Uncle Ted. Ted was the youngest, a slight, nervous fellow whom our aunts always spoke of in either sympathetic or frustrated tones, the sum of their comments translating to a shrug: "Mother's eggs were stale by the time Teddy was hatched." When Ted came back from Korea, he had a tic that would never still and that metal buckle in his skull locking in whatever memories of war had left him so trembly. To me, Teddy just seemed an average guy, an after-thought baby tacked onto the end of a large, quick-witted family (an unenviable position). He lived with Grandma Julia until his forties, when he surprised everyone by getting married and staying married long enough to father a son.

The youngest Stonich daughter, Mardi, married a local boy, Lew, described in the oxymoronic as a jovial Finn. Though he'd married in, Lew was the uncle we saw the most. Dad would haul me along to visit him out on Johnson Lake, where Lew's old mobile home was parked but never plumbed or improved, kept rustic to discourage females. He and my Dad would have a bump and a beer, a bump being three fingers of whiskey, neat, enough to paste my lightweight father into his lawn chair.

Most blood uncles are only murky memories. All seemed so *old*, and most had gone off to become businessmen, returning only sporadically for visits or funerals. Dad's sisters drifted off to marry men from elsewhere. Aunt Mary's first husband was such a long-harbored secret that I was in my thirties before I learned of him, a dashing, high-rolling architect from California who was either abusive or alcoholic and probably both. They'd lived unmoored and fast, had dined at Hearst Castle and spent a few tumultuous years traveling before divorcing. Divorce was relegated to the family closet of Unmentioned Things; it simply wasn't *done* by Catholics. Another aunt's husband was murdered by his mistress, an event that was vehemently never spoken of.

All five of our aunts returned home each summer. I recall them best during the 1960s, when they filled the large pine-paneled cabin on White Iron Lake. The kitchen was loud as a chicken run with everyone trying to get their points and arguments across, along with jokes, gossip from town, discussions of best sellers, and cries over bad hands of bridge. Back when they could put it away, there were gin and vodka cocktails and always a lot of lemons. There was the occasional guiltily puffed cigarette on the porch, though never when Grandma Julia was around. Arguments about politics were often started by Dad and ended by his going fishing. The Aunts might not have agreed on everything, but they all got very nonpartisan when recalling poor, dear Jack Kennedy, growing gin maudlin until they were sidetracked with the details of Jackie's new wardrobe or her antics in Greece.

The Aunts wore pedal pushers, Keds slip-ons, and cat-wing RayBans. All were eager to see what Aunt Mary would wear. She was worldly, spoke French, and never talked about her wealth, though behind her back everyone else did. Each year she sent our mother a care package. Opening it was an event. I remember a sheath dress covered in gold spangles that my size-ten mother could never have squeezed into no matter how many star jumps with Jack LaLanne. Things like nice soaps came in the box, interesting costume jewelry, a cloisonné candy dish, a cut-glass bowl, evening dresses. A blouse covered in tiny silk bows and a snakeskin belt. Expensive things, never anything practical.

When swimming, the Aunts wore bathing caps with straps and posed on the dock for the requisite beauty-legs photo like a line of petite, squinting Rockettes (the tallest was five foot two). They first outlived all their brothers, then began outliving their husbands, and now have sadly and inevitably begun to outlive each other. When I bought the land, four of the five were alive, now only one. Not all of their endings have been easy. Three became addled by Alzheimer's, and another lived trapped in her own shell for a dozen years after a stroke left her wheelchair bound and maddeningly unable to speak. Our surviving aunt, Helen, still has her marbles and remembers when they were their younger, witty, vibrant selves. In Ely, the Stonich girls are remembered, though more recall my grandmother, who was more or less a fixture in town.

I once did a reading at an Ely bookstore, where I arrived to a surprisingly full house. Not quite my typical audience, the median age looked to be over seventy, and at least one attendee had a walker. After the reading, the usual Q-and-A began, but no one seemed at all curious about the book. Instead they offered comments and little stories about my family, mostly about my grandparents. One stout, blue-haired lady piped up, "Your grandmother made me a wool skirt in 1940, and now it's braided into a rug in my mud room." A shy miner stepped forward: "I was in Korea with your Uncle Teddy," prompting several men to nod knowingly. A chipper, very old mason offered, "I tuck-pointed Joe

Stonich's chimney and poured him a sidewalk in barter for the suit I got married in." He tugged at the equally ancient woman at his side as if to corroborate his story.

As people were filing past to say good-bye, a shaky woman took my elbow, her voice low. She told me that one day during the worst of the Depression, she'd been outside the butcher shop with her mother, who was counting the coins in her palm, comparing what she had to the prices in the window. "Then Julia Stonich came by, and without a blink, your grandmother opened her purse and slipped two dollar bills into my mother's hand." The woman shook her head. "It was probably all *she* had to feed her own with."

That geriatric audience telling me such stories was easily the most gratifying event I'd ever done. Not a book was sold.

↜

My family, once so much a part of this place, has physically vanished, and when they fade from memory, it will be almost as if they never were. I'm the only one of my sisters who has kept the Stonich name, which I've now dragged back north to plant like a flag. If we take root here, if it works, in another hundred years maybe some curious great-grandchild will be peering back into this time to look at now, just as I am looking back to then.

Twelve

I was beginning to relish single life, having lived with one man or another with little or no breathing room between since my early twenties. For the first time, I was independent and had no intention of becoming the sort of woman who cannot be truly happy until she mutters the barfable "You complete me." Single felt as good as trading shoes for flip-flops on the first warm day. Still, there were times when I looked around my lovely building site and felt a little bereft, like when you're watching a good movie or a sunset and it seems a shame there's no one to elbow. Yes, single was definitely the best route, and I determined that if I *had* to grow old alone, I would at least do so gracefully, without too many regrets or cats.

I'd be manless but happy—or at least content.

For a few weeks, I was childless as well. Sam and Terry were away on the big trip they'd been planning for years. Sam had wanted to go to Japan ever since I brought home an illustrated guide called *Today's Japan* and a stuffed sumo wrestler doll when he was little. He got very interested in anime and read novelty books of weird Japanese inventions. He went around imitating the accents in Kurosawa films, repeating most-useful phrases for tourists from *Japanese Made Easy*, sounding just like an angry samurai warrior would when asking directions to the nearest train station or karaoke bar. On special occasions, he didn't want steak, he wanted sushi.

Sam and Terry had been buddies since he was eight, when we'd become neighbors in St. Paul. By eighteen, Sam was wild to visit Japan and took off for Tokyo under Terry's wing, though by this time he was taller by a head.

I took the opportunity to spend time in Ely in a leisurely way. The tourists were gone, and the place had settled back to normal. I hung around the library and the history center, looking up old records and reading. I spent the rest of my time just nosing around town and eavesdropping in the coffee shop, laundromat, or Dee's if it wasn't too busy, when I could talk the pull-tab lady into playing cribbage.

Lars had put roof trusses atop the main cabin. His construction leftovers included a pile of short four-foot scraps of 8 × 8-inch-square pine timbers. He made use of them and designed a footbridge to span the swampy area between the shoreline and the granite island, throwing it in as a sort of gift-with-purchase, like a Lincoln Log kit. There were enough dovetailed lengths for three cribs to anchor the bridge. Cribs are interlocking timber corrals filled with large stones to keep them anchored, typically used in much larger projects to support bridges or boathouses, but in this case to support a footbridge and a 125-pound woman.

It was my last trip north before winter. Out at the land, the structures were taking shape. The log walls and roof beams had grayed to a soft driftwood. We'd decided to leave the roof off for the winter so the interior walls and trusses could gray as well. On the day I was leaving, I stopped by to find that Lars had cut openings for the windows and door. He'd also built a heavy hand-hewn picnic table and placed it at the crest of the rocky slope to the lake.

I had a meal sitting at the new table. It didn't matter that I was alone or that it was just a meat pasty eaten straight from its wrapper and dabbed at a torn-open packet of ketchup; I was dining *alfresco* at my very own place in the woods. Autumn was full on. The bugs were gone, and the fallen leaves were dry underfoot and loud as Doritos. Those still on the trees were thrumming loose from branches to join the eastward curtain of wind, slowly opening the view to the lake across the wooded slope. On the floor of the roofless cabin, eddies of fallen birch leaves swirled like schools of guppies and sawdust lapped at the walls. I suddenly didn't want to go home. I wanted to stay and see it through until the last leaf was down, but it was time.

Back in the city, I settled in to await our urban autumn, to watch another round of leaves fall, this time from my office window.

Just as the rhythm of days fell into a pattern, I found myself connecting with a neighbor I'd been friendly with for years. His son and Sam had attended the same day camp together. It turned out Butch had recently become single himself and didn't have any pending warrants, so we went out. By Christmas we'd advanced a step, and I kept a pair of earplugs at his weekend house. Butch ran a busy company and didn't have loads of leisure, but no matter, since my own winter was taken up with work. Butch's schedule was difficult to keep track of. He was often flying off here and there, and when he was around, his inner clock was cockeyed from international travel. Much of the time, he functioned with cell phone glued to his ear, telecommuting between offices in two separate towns. He also lived in a trio of houses, each roughly an hour from the next, which meant I rarely knew where he was, and he never knew where his favorite sweater was. We saw each other when we could.

Winter came and went. While fall comes early up north, spring comes maddeningly late, dragging two weeks or more behind southern Minnesota. It would be late mud season before I was able to get to the land again. Lars, with a more rugged vehicle, was able to get there sooner.

He found the cabin not quite as he'd left it. The whole building was leaning. We had assumed that the site we'd chosen was packed dirt over ledge rock, and since the building sits not on a traditional foundation but on skids, there'd been no digging or drilling down that might have revealed there was indeed no ledge rock.

For having such a small footprint, the cabin is a petite monster weight-wise, its walls overbuilt by any standard, with heavy square timbers and subflooring two inches thick. Lars had come to install windows, but when he found soil beginning to give way under the weight of one of the skids and trickle down the slope, he immediately went to work building a log retaining wall five feet east of the cabin. Then he began the arduous task of filling it in with loads of gravel. I didn't realize he'd done so much extra work until much later since he'd never mentioned it, nor had he charged any extra, which seemed very un-contractor-like. I already doubted that he would break even on the project, and this extra work confirmed my suspicion.

I couldn't get up to see it myself as I was driving my way through eastern states on a grueling, unsuccessful work-related trip, during which I sprained my ankle and contracted a nasty bronchial infection. While on the road, Butch's phone calls grew erratic and constrained, making me wonder if he was overworked or just jet lagged. The guy was spread awfully thin, I reasoned. Or maybe it was me. I was anxious about work and realized I was going to have to sell my house. My stomach got up to its old tricks, and I went back to my old habits of Rolaids and ginger ale.

Plans to meet Butch's mother kept falling through, and when we tried to schedule a trip north, one business trip or another kept pushing it back. Then, just as things were looking a little brighter, we were driving somewhere one morning when his cell phone rang. After a lot of shifting in his seat and mumbling, Butch said, as if I were not sitting a foot away, "Yes, I'm alone."

Seems he had fallen back into an ongoing love-hate snarl with a woman who will remain his first cousin, though being blood relatives was "no biggie," Butch insisted, since she was past child-bearing age. Date over.

As it turned out, Sam was a far better judge of the men I dated than I was. Of those few that were around long enough for him to meet, he had them silently pegged: Egotistical and Weird, Charity Case, and Awkward to the Core. I might have saved myself wasted time by merely asking what descriptions he'd settled on.

I was doubly motivated to move off the same city block where both a former husband and a cheating former boyfriend resided. I'd lived on our street nineteen years in three different houses, and it was clearly time to go, though I would see less of Sam, who lived half time with his dad next door in the house he grew up in, coming and going freely around the fence that cordoned off one parent from the other, an arrangement that had been great for Sam though not quite the optimal distance for divorced parents.

I spit-shined my house and put it on the market. In the meantime, I could at least get out of town. Because of spring rains, there were a few cancellations at Rustic Resort, and I was able to get a last-minute, low-season deal on a cabin for the week. And while the land didn't yet have a habitable building to stay in, it seemed that north really was becoming a retreat.

Hauling a few tools to the land, I was surprised to find the outhouse had been re-erected on-site. At least something was going right. The inspector, aptly named John, had been out and left his stamped certificate from the county and a note that it was all "good to go." On a little round of pine, I wood-burned the word "Bog," which is what my Scottish friends charmingly call the toilet, and nailed it to the door. Now we had two bogs. I found a lidded, mouse-proof grain bucket to store toilet paper in, stocked a can of Raid and a flyswatter, and dug a magazine rack from storage along with vintage copies of *National Geographic* and *Reader's Digest.* I settled in for my first indoor read.

The place was transforming. No longer a parcel or just a building site, no longer raw land, it was beginning to feel downright homey.

My house sold unexpectedly fast in a good-news/bad-news scenario with the buyer wanting quick possession, which left me furiously house hunting for a stressful month. With only two weeks to spare, I found a great old duplex: more good/bad news in that it had only half the storage of the old place. I quickly had to gather and pack the rest of my hoarded cabin things and hire a truck to take it all north to the Mayflower trailer.

I wanted to get everything settled so that I could enjoy a long-anticipated trip at the end of the summer, a yoga retreat in California with a good friend. Lars promised the cabin would be finished soon after my return, maybe even by September. The bit of straw Butch had knocked out of me was slowly beginning to fill back in, and I'd eased up some on kicking myself over my bad choices.

I began unpacking and putting my new home in order. It was a hot summer in St. Paul, and the whole of July felt thick, something to survive. I starting working in the air-conditioned public library downtown, joining the ranks of homeless. I was supposed to be reading about pro–sport fishing for a project I was researching but kept getting distracted in the history stacks, drawn to books on the Iron Range. I'd never been much interested in history; I liked it informal and coated in glossy entertainment, preferring the *story* part. Movies are good; cartoons are better. Do I need to know more about the Civil War than is in *Gone with the Wind*, more about the Napoleonic high seas than can be gleaned from *Master and Commander*, or anything about life in the north that Rocky or Bullwinkle cannot impart? I loved historical novels for their descriptions of rooms and furniture and clothes, accurate or not. When curious about the actual factual past, I prefer books with titles like *The Very Bloody History of Britain without the Boring Bits*, *The Wordy Shipmates*, or *Four Score . . . and More!* Minnesota history held little thrall for me until I become steward of a tiny chunk of it. Until then, I was happy enough with Paul Bunyan digging out Lake Superior as a watering hole for Babe the Blue Ox, creating lakes with his size-104 boots, and leveling forests just by tromping about and the Ojibwe warrior hero Nanabozho (Naniboujou), who saved the remaining trees from Paul's clodhoppers by fighting with him for forty days and forty nights, finally killing him with a big fish and a pancake. Right?

There's tons of fakelore in northern Minnesota. Leif Erickson rowing over to Duluth from Norway in the year AD 1000? The Kensington Runestone is widely known as a hoax, but a sports team named the Vikings does sound much more menacing than the Voyageurs, which only conjures up a vision of swarthy guys eating pâté or singing "Alouette." If the Viking lore hadn't proliferated, Monday night cheers would be led by a little guy with a paddle wearing a tasseled cap instead of horns. Surely the voyageurs were tougher than they looked. By any account, voyageuring was dangerous and backbreaking; a job posting might have read, "Guys built like bulldogs: become a human pack mule and paddle slave."

I was more interested in the later years, the time of my grandfather's arrival, when big men with names like Weyerhaeuser, Hill, and Backus oozed in from the big cities with their handlebar mustaches and homburg hats. When they saw the timber to be logged, the lumber barons grew nearly animated, mustaches a-twitch, and snapped to action. The first order of the day was to lay railways so they could then cut down Minnesota, haul it out, and sell it, which they did between 1830 and 1930, when around 70 percent of the state was shorn bald (today only two percent of Minnesota forest is considered old growth) and the timber was either floated downriver or trundled off by train, mostly to eastern states. Aerial photos from the 1920s show the Lake Vermilion area, tens of thousands of acres, reduced to pathetic stumpage, our land included. What is now the Boundary Waters wasn't spared either, save a few islands too inconveniently located to mow over. Did these lumber corporations use proper logging practices? No. Nor did they employ any reforestation programs. Nary a tree was planted in their wake, but even worse, loggers took only the tree trunks, leaving mountains of branches called "slash" to dry, and the slash become tinder over the vast clearings where there were no longer any trees to divert or slow spreading fires or the winds they rode in on. Fledgling hamlets and towns across the Iron Range burned to the ground. In 1908, Chisholm was incinerated. The city of Virginia burned *twice.* Looking at the pictures, I can only wonder how the industrialists got away with so many crimes against nature, and I puzzle over how one comes to possess such boundless temerity. "Because they were raging shitheads" is how Juri put it.

It's hard to envision the desiccated lands and towns or imagine the impact on the Ojibwe who lived there—losing their livelihoods, their woodland existence, their hunting and ricing grounds, and their fishing waters, powerless while watching their environment ravaged for profit and slowly raked away and into the white men's coffers.

⌒

Precious minerals had already been explored by prospectors all over northern St. Louis County. The original gold diggers came and found jack and left. Some, considered fools, stayed on, and being patient and looking stupid paid off for them in 1893 when gold was finally discovered on Rainy Lake and the Little American Mine was established. Meanwhile other mineral hunters who'd failed to find precious metals did discover something else:

a tsunami of ore deposits drifting just under the three iron ranges. Lucky, lucky, lucky.

Another wave of big men barreled in to start up the mines, managerial types with lackeys trailing behind at a safe distance, gingerly lugging a *lot* of dynamite. They landgrabbed the most viable mining land plus anything else they could get their hands on—swamp, bog, lake, you name it. From afar, the bosses sat counting the seconds on their gold pocket watches between explosions. Since the land had been conveniently scalped by logging and fires, mining exploration went off with few hitches and to great success. Our own land is an example, pitted with blasted test sites, dozens of depressions the size of barnyard troughs or larger.

An immigrant's first view upon arriving, depending on the season, would have been either of stumps and mud, stumps and dust, stumps and frozen mud, or stumps and snow. These newcomers wore yet another set of hats, the shabby haberdashery of the working class: Welsh tweed caps and battered Italian fedoras and whatever mad headgear the Finns and Bohunks had donned when embarking from the old country. Most came to escape the oppression and poverty back home, where there were ugly wars and plenty of tyranny. Finland, as it was ruled by the Swedes, was no picnic, particularly for laborers or free thinkers, which included a good portion of the population. Here in the land of free speech, they could air their communist leanings and get all atheist without being too offensive or getting murdered for it. Hope for a better life drove them here to about the only other place in the world just as cold as Finland but with arguably better jobs. These immigrants, along with legions from other small

European countries like Montenegro, formed labor forces that would not labor for too many years in bad conditions before realizing there was oppression here, too, in the great nation of America. Some began revolting, forming unions, rabble-rousing, and making general nuisances of themselves to the guys in the fanciest hats, the investors and industrialists. From a distance, it's easy to see why communism looked so good to so many at that time. In theory it still does, especially while watching *Reds* on a digital flat screen costing well over the annual income of an early miner.

The past on the Iron Range is harsh and full of villains and heroes, good guys and bad, but mostly just a lot of plain folks looking to get by. If you were a Native during the heaviest of the mass immigration between the 1870s and 1920s, life was not good. Several unfair treaties were signed in exchange that the Ojibwe might retain their least-valuable lands, and the rest was purloined. Government schools were hastily built with the overall goal to culturally reeducate, their credo being, and this actually written down, "Kill the Indian, Save the Man!" Knock some white into them was the idea. The schools were notorious for abuse and wretched conditions, though the Indian school near Tower, built for the Nett Lake and Bois Forte bands on the eastern shore of Lake Vermilion, was allegedly somewhat less awful if only because the Vermilion school was staffed by Native teachers who allowed children to speak their native language in the dormitories and who tended not to punish them when they slipped in the classroom. They also had access to the Ojibwe grapevine that connected teachers to the children's parents and relatives, meaning most kids were not completely cut off from news of home and thus were a little less isolated and many of the students and teachers were even related. In 1910, the year my father was born, the population of the school peaked at over a hundred students.

Julia visited the school a few times to show the Native domestics teacher how to operate a sewing machine. I tried getting her to describe the place once, but she claimed she didn't remember much, just that it was like any run-down school, though the name of a particular girl had stuck with her always: Louisa Blue Sky.

Though my grandmother lived to ninety-nine and was a fixture in my life until I was nearly thirty, I knew little about her family history, only that her parents were caterers and that she was born in Mottling, Austria, and immigrated as a toddler to America with her father, Franc Tancig; mother, Marija Mak; and several siblings. Julia learned English at school and spoke Slovene and German at home, often translating for her mother and older siblings.

∽

At home, I stuck close to the one air conditioner in my back-bedroom office. After ten hours in front of a computer each day, ennui began seeping in. I found myself listlessly surfing the 'Net. I should have been content, but I'd run out of pathetic Internet dating stories to entertain married friends with and make them feel grateful for not being me, so I tentatively prepared for another round of online dating, though this time would be different. My bar was raised. I changed my profile to reflect what I felt I deserved, not what I'd settle for. If a date was awful, I would walk—no excuses, no Minnesota nice.

Just *one* more go, then I'd unplug. I leisurely checked the site for a few weeks, but nobody piqued my interest, no one seemed compelling. Then, just as I was about to close up shop, a profile I hadn't seen before popped up. This new guy looked fresh and seemed as genuine as one can in a few assigned paragraphs and answers to canned questions. He could construct a sentence and liked junk shopping. Of course, what he *wasn't* was equally important: born-again, Republican, or short. He didn't talk himself up much. In fact, his profile was completely devoid of that underlying "the wonder of me" tone that colors so many of them. Even his online moniker was modest: Bonhomie. There was the photo to consider; he definitely had a chin, and his eyes and mouth were set in roughly the right places. He had *dimples!* And if it turned out he had hair under that cap, all the better.

I'd learned not to bother with any pre-date e-mail chitchat wherein guys blather on with Googled quips, trying to brand themselves as Really Something before the date, as if not fore-seeing that they would actually be expected to converse, or what they might consider improv. But the reality is there's no way to glean character or any detail over the Internet unless the person is performing a striptease on Skype. The new rules included "no time wasted." If he doesn't have potential, get out fast, mercenary, efficient.

I examined the fresh guy's profile one more time. In regard to the question of politics, he'd mused, "How do Carville and Matalin do it?" Ah, I thought. I'm *not* the only one puzzling. Under "What celebrity do you most resemble?" he responded, "I'm told I look like one of the guys in the Lipitor commercial. I hope I'm the one with low cholesterol." I made the date.

Thirteen

Lipitor Guy showed up at the restaurant on time, getting points for that (what dating had come to) and extra points for being terribly handsome. And he had all his own hair, which was perfectly silvered at the temples, as if he might run for office after cocktails. He was wearing shoes, not trainers, and a dark gray uber-fabric T-shirt that clung over a good chest and a fit set of arms. We shook hands. Jon, Sarah.

"Huh."

"Hmm."

Ever wary on first dates, especially after previous calamities, I took a while to relax. He seemed ever-so-slightly wary himself and for some reason insisted on sitting to my right, which required some chair wrangling and disruption. Was he *that* fussy about where he sat? Did he have some obsessive-compulsive disorder that prevented him from sitting on *anyone's* left, ever? Why did the good-looking ones always come with some glitch? He certainly smelled right enough, and I was soon leaning into his explanation of the musical chairs. Simply, a tumor and the bones of his inner ear had been removed years before in a procedure he described briefly in nonmedical terms. He was able to make light of losing an eardrum, which must have been a heavy loss for a musician. While I was taking a good look at the dimples, he joked about his surgery so that, looking back much later, I would think, "He had me at melon baller."

Being one drum short of a bongo set was nothing. From all indications, he lived up to his profile alias, Bonhomie—a good guy. I deemed him not to be dangerous and, after our drink, let him walk me home, where we sat on my front porch and discussed the etymology of a single word for a half hour, and when I had to break out the laptop to Wiki other esoteric things we were equally curious about, we knew there would be a second date.

Appropriately, our second date involved a game of Scrabble, this time on his front porch. We were a little too preoccupied to play very well. I let him win, and he let me kiss him. This one definitely had potential.

A casual third date was followed by a hiatus during which I was away on my long-anticipated yoga week at a retreat center on the California coast in Big Sur, the original seat of hippiedom and New Age plinkyness. While I was there, a volley of e-mails revealed Jon could write an entertaining paragraph and was a stickler for grammar, which only made my knees weaker.

As soon as my yoga mates shut their eyes during meditation session, I'd slip away, unable to concentrate, and compulsively check my e-mail, an activity definitely frowned upon by the docents. But what if Jon had left me a message during the Om chants or Pranayama breathing?

Whenever I heard the one man in class referred to as a "yogi," I fought to keep a straight face, expecting Boo-Boo to come swinging through with his pic-a-nic basket as we down-dogged or balanced in tree pose. I could barely keep from falling out of headstand when we women were called "yoginis."

Many guests were from big cities, and like me, they just needed a break and some quiet. Others were diehards, like the radical beyond-vegan parents in the line to get our dinner trays. They were consuming only raw fruits, vegetables, juices, and nuts during their stay at the center. Their two little boys, adorable but zipper-thin, made me want to slip them cheese dogs and Snickers.

Many guests kept to strict agendas that wrung every drop of spirituality out of each moment, intent on blissing out 24/7. The lawns were flocked with people doing tai chi, quietly chanting, fingering talismans, or just standing around on their heads. One day I was hula-hooping near the pool and reading a book when a woman wearing a wreath edged up to inquire, "What are you doing?"

"Hula-hooping," I replied, "and reading a book?"

"Yes, but what are you *doing?*"

I thought of Jon with his deep admiration of facts. His e-mails were inquisitive and charming. His down-to-earth perspective made me think of lactose-tolerant midwesterners who ate deep-fried food on sticks.

Returning from my retreat, relaxed from all the yoga and limp from the mineral baths, I forgot to be guarded and skeptical and impulsively invited Jon up for the Labor Day weekend, when the cabin was slated to be finished. Lars had reported that the doors were hung, the windows were in, and finishing touches were being made.

I'd never spent the night at the cabin myself, not even camping, and now I was going with a relative stranger with whom I'd spent a total of twelve hours on four dates. What was I thinking? For one thing, I hadn't seen him with his shirt off, and for another, The Lake was *my* place, my haven, my sanctuary, but beyond that, it had come to embody my independence after too many years of none. This Labor Day was meant to be my maiden voyage, a sort of christening: "I am mistress of all I survey," *ad nauseam.*

Hadn't I *just* given up on men? I hardly knew Jon; he wasn't exactly an open book. He was taciturn, as Julia would describe anyone hesitant to reveal himself, a trait she admired. Jon didn't hang out his prizes or try to impress, but then neither did he hang out his dirty laundry or flash any warnings. What had been revealed so far had been pleasant, but might pleasantness mask some major character flaw? As far as I knew, *Bonhomie* could have been a sociopath or NASCAR fan. My first visits to his house had left me vaguely uneasy until I pinpointed what was wrong—no books! When I finally asked, he explained they'd been in storage since he'd remodeled. Okay, so his books were only out of sight—but *what* books?

Soon enough I'd know plenty. I'd be alone in the woods with this guy for four days and four very dark nights. Recalling all the sage dating advice from relatives, I remembered "Get him good and drunk" and bought two bottles of wine and invited him over on a school night. For three hours, we yakked about anything and nothing and never opened the second bottle. I'd forgotten about the whole exercise until he left. He passed the getting drunk test with flying colors by not getting drunk.

Then there was: "Tackle a project together." I already knew Jon was handy enough to wield a Sawzall and do minor plumbing but was prudent enough to hire someone else for floor refinishing (only a fool would tackle his own), but it was too soon to recruit him for any sort of domestic task, so I asked for help regarding a computer problem, of which I have legion. His points accrued when he didn't lose patience with me like the IT guy or bump me aside like Sam (who, to be fair, has also been known to roll my office chair away gently, as if sending an elder out on an ice floe). Jon straightened out a few of my file gaffes, then offered to set me up on a better e-mail system, plugging me into the one he used, in the process becoming privy to my password, which I took to mean we were going steady.

We packed up the wagon, strapped a futon on top, and I drove north with crossed fingers. Halfway there, we passed a gleaming milk truck and were startled by its reflection of a giant balloon quivering atop the car. Wind had breached the plastic-zipper futon bag and filled it to bursting with air. For the remainder of the trip, we listened to the bag flutter and flap and tried not to think of its effect on the gas mileage, amusing ourselves by watching the expressions of other drivers puzzling over our odd topside spectacle.

From the main road, there are two approaches to the land, both unpaved and rugged. One is a trail once called the Tower-Ely Road, though it's barely pickup passable and now (of course) called something else. Rusted bits of metal along the ditches could be vintage oil pans or mufflers sheared off by the hump with grass that camouflages jutting bits of stone. Our neighbor Mac had had two tires punctured during a single journey of just over a mile. The other route, longer but less harrowing, begins on a county road named for a respected local man who had tromped or canoed every township and section in the northern half of the county during the forties and fifties, a forest ranger, land broker, and sometimes amateur historian and ethnographer. His notations of various historic Native sites and points of interest are on many survey maps of the region. I was thrilled to discover that copies of the maps could be acquired through the Minnesota History Center library. His son Bill was the avuncular real estate broker who'd showed me so many places for sale and finally gave me the tip regarding our mine-owned parcels. That county road is a well-tended wide gravel ribbon that rises and falls from ridges of high pine down to the water level of roadside ponds. The turnoff to Lake Road is no wider than a driveway, down a sloping blind hill you wouldn't notice if you weren't looking. The maximum speed limit is twenty miles per hour; much faster will undo a front-end alignment. The mile-plus drive from the county road to our driveway can take fifteen minutes even if nothing has fallen across the road.

Jon was likely wondering just how far into the boonies I was dragging him, but eventually we turned at the dead pine and the wooden sign onto the cabin drive. We pulled up to the slight rise overlooking the piney plateau. We had arrived. From the car, the little clutch of buildings looked like a pioneer homestead, as if the historical society had been by and clicked their heels three times. It was finished! Phase one of my dream was complete, and completely charming. The cabin had doors and windows, the outhouse had a metal roof to match the cabin, and the ribs of the timber-frame shed stood like an ark-in-progress. Everything was swept and tidy, no sign of construction mess.

On the long drive up, I'd wondered if I hadn't overhyped the place to Jon. For weeks I'd teased him with "The lichen is amazing," or "Just wait till you see the crapper," and a dozen other come-ons. Jon might have been expecting the moon. Looking around as if through his eyes—as if I'd just been dropped there not knowing what to expect—I saw then, and might even have said aloud, "It's beautiful."

It really was, and more than I'd hoped for.

Once we examined every corner, wall, and window, we christened the place with a beer, and I stopped jumping up and down long enough to commence playing Cabin! for real. We eased the futon from its giant deflated condom on top of the car, carried it flopping over our heads, and jammed it up into the loft. There was a bed—with a roof over it!

We outfitted the place with stuff from the Mayflower, where the stash could furnish the little cabin and a few others. Over the long holiday weekend, we fished, played cribbage, swam, hiked, paddled around, and sat in front of smoky campfires until our kisses tasted like Slim Jims. In one shades-of-*The-African-Queen* moment after an evening skinny dip, Jon pulled little leeches off me, and we fell in love.

⌒

Wonderful. Really great, in fact. But would Jon take to the land as he took to me, or would he come to see the place as a weekend maintenance albatross? I couldn't expect him to feel as welded onto the place as I was. Would he share some sort of stewardship along with me, or at least humor me in my endeavor? I can't say that if I were in his shoes I'd have been totally thrilled if my new love came glued to a lifelong, high-maintenance project with soaring property taxes. Everywhere you looked, something needed doing or fixing: brush burned, stumps grubbed, paths cleared, trees cut, etc. I saw how it could be overwhelming. A future with me must've looked like a lot of work, weekends spent in work boots and flannel shirts, predetermined and predictable. Would this place wind up being fifty acres of ball and chain?

The building project we eventually tackled together was to design and construct windows for the little fish house, which we decided should become a sleeping cabin, so much more comfortable than climbing in and out of the tiny loft in the main cabin, where just making the bed involved a whacked funny bone at best and a contusion at worst.

Making custom windows was no easy task given that every opening Rory had framed was slightly off (like him), each measuring a markedly different size from the next. The project became a challenge of patience and math skills, traits I do not possess. I bought panels of a polycarbonate channeled plastic, the kind newer greenhouses are clad in, much lighter weight than glass, unbreakable, and, as it turns out, bear proof. The downside, which I now see as an upside, is that while light comes through, sharp details don't, just shapes and colors, an impressionist's view.

In my landlord's well-lit, dry basement back home, we fired up the table saw, and over the course of several weekends, Jon chewed a pencil and measured and cut, humming while I held things or tidied up. Even in the city, I was guilty of recruiting my boyfriend like a Habitat volunteer when we might have gone to a gallery opening or to hear a band or maybe lazed around Sunday mornings with the crossword and coffee. I swept sawdust and plastic dust and nodded encouragement. When one of the plastic panels skidded over the running table-saw blade and was badly scratched, we laughed it off, joking that at least there would be one visible flaw in our otherwise perfect collaboration. With the help of excessive weather stripping, the finished windows fit well enough, opening outward and up to hook to the eaves to save precious room inside. They also act as broad awnings, so if one is left open in rain, there's no worry. The outside mount also protects the screens from falling branches and curious squirrels.

The scratch made by the table saw is only noticeable when you're prone in bed, a reminder that Jon and I get on swell even while toiling in a dirty basement, where blame for what goes wrong is not assigned to the nearest person but to the sonofabitching table saw. As it turned out, Jon didn't seem to mind all the cabin maintenance. As long as he got to fish, nothing seemed to puncture his good humor. This could work, I thought.

Fourteen

The buildings were up, but there was still plenty to do around the place. I know which end of the hammer to hold and can do a little finish carpentry, though my framing skills are limited to picture framing. I'm not Rosie the Riveter, but I wanted to contribute. We soon realized that working off the grid has specific limitations, bearing little relation to projects taken on in the plumbed and wired world of civilization. Working outdoors with no electricity or work surfaces and a half-hour drive to the nearest hardware store can turn the simplest do-it-yourself project into a make-do-it-yourself challenge.

Woefully ill equipped, I didn't realize that all my existing tools would be rendered null. I owned lightweight plug-in girly tools: a silly drill, a weak sander, a sissy saw. My toolbox of screwdrivers, hammers, and wrenches might as well be labeled Fisher-Price. I needed new cordless, heavier versions of everything. In the aisles of Fleet Farm, I looked at gas-operated generators, brush cutters, and chain saws, lifting and dropping price tags and flinching in advance at the idea of running power tools with hand-yanked ignitions, blue smoke, and whirring blades.

The battery-operated chain saw is a purchase I may never live down, now nicknamed "Lady Schick." If I use all my weight and an additional backup battery, Lady and I can chaw through a young poplar trunk in six to ten minutes. By the time I squeak *timber!*, my neighbors with their smoking Husqvarnas and Stihls have already cut copses of trees as if mowing stalks of celery.

Looking around at all that needed doing and weighing the difficulties ahead, it's no wonder I contracted a case of dwindling confidence. I was able to clean up, stain logs, do finishing work— and that was about it.

The rustic, wide, rough plank floors in either building weren't adequate. They were rustic, all right, with uneven cracks of light that indicated, yes indeed, that's how all the battalions of bugs and bats were getting in. I cleared both buildings and had Rory come out to install plywood subfloors and four-inch smooth floorboards of tightly grained tamarack, which would, Rory insisted, outlast us all, sounding remarkably like my father. It seemed I was constantly being reminded of the enduring sturdiness of everything in our little compound as it related to the mortality of our weak, flesh-clad frames. It made me wish for a mobile home delivered complete, down to the knobs and cushions, the sort of structure I would live to see crumble.

Rory did a beautiful job, and when it came time to sand and finish, he took off, dragging his generator behind him. Forgetting my own credo that only a fool would tackle their own floorfinishing, I gathered sanding blocks and papers of varying grits, tack cloths, brushes, stain, polyurethane, and a sleeping bag. For two days, I hand sanded on my knees while pine chaff floated in through the screens, a green grit that mingled with the fine wood dust, gunking up the sandpaper and my face mask, effective as a doily so that I blew Kermit-colored snot. Wishing for a roaring Shop-Vac, I ineffectually skidded my battery-operated Dustbuster around (no wonder bears hate them), resorting to a child's broom, which only raised more dust.

I slept in the back of the station wagon, which would have been uncomfortable even if my bones weren't already grousing from crouching and kneeling all day. I spent the third morning staining and varnishing, with only the radio to talk to.

WELY, run by the local Bois Forte Band of Ojibwe, airs a Slovene language show, Native news programming, Twins baseball games (sounding identical to those aired in the 1960s), a call-in message board for campers in the BWCA, lost-and-found announcements, want ads, and music programming with everything from bluegrass to waltz to punk. Recorded ads for local businesses are reminiscent of old AM radio spots, often with *da up nort'* accent exaggerated. The *Polka Pal Don* show had aired every Saturday morning since I'd learned to walk, and after Don died, it was revived as the *Old Town Polka Show*, with the same Frankie Yankovic tunes like "Beavers Polka," dedicated to such folks as Otto and Elsa celebrating their thirty-fifth or for Arno at the nursing home turning ninety-five years young. The only other static-free stations were the CBC and a French-language news station from Ontario, but only WELY sounded like an open phone line from yesteryear, as if someone in the 1960s forgot to put the receiver back on the hook.

I sanded and tacked the floor between coats, bobbing along to mazurkas in the morning and seventies rock in the afternoon, happily unaware of the fumes until I had finished singing a rousing off-key rendition of "Bohemian Rhapsody" at the top of my lungs and could feel the headache coming like a fist. On my to-buy list I wrote "respirator" and on my wish list added "generator."

I gained new respect for Rory and Lars for being able to work tirelessly in adverse outdoor conditions, seemingly immune to the heat, mosquitoes, black flies, frostbite, and fatigue. They were tough up-north versions of Norwegian bachelor farmers, sort of lone-wolf bachelor loggers. Their homes are on a large, female-free chunk of land that's been in the family for generations, where they can do what they want without anybody breathing down their necks, without the government telling them what they can or cannot do.

Such isolated living seemed sometimes to affect their communication skills. Rory's hearing was fine; he was only listening impaired when it came to vital instructions regarding specific tasks. Or maybe he was just too busy talking to listen. One day while he was working on the fish house, Terry dropped by, and upon being introduced, Rory launched into long soliloquies, including details of a part-by-part car restoration he was working on, a diatribe on why the economy was tanking (liberals), and a protracted story of a recent malady in which his testicles swelled to the size of cantaloupes.

We spoke at length about a design for the solar shed, which would open from one side to access the batteries and controls, with a covered open space on the opposite side to stack wood. Rory constructed it at the sawmill, and when it was delivered to the site and plunked down, I could only stare, speechless. It was completely ass-backwards, bearing no resemblance to the plan. It was a 2 × 4-foot closet with a useless porch and door on the wrong side, with nowhere to store wood. I'd requested 6 × 6, which indeed were the dimensions *of the roof.* Along with my new closet, I got an expensive lesson in learning to be explicit, Rory got a check, and I still didn't have a shed.

Rory had been deeply impressed by a documentary called *Alone in the Wilderness,* by Dick Proenneke, a city fellow who went rogue during his fifties, leaving civilization and the lower forty-eight states for the Alaskan wilds to live far off the grid and, as the title suggests, very much alone. Proenneke's survival depended largely on being clever, and fortunately he had nothing but time to think stuff up. The trek on foot into his valley was many rugged miles, so he didn't transport much in the way of weight, maybe an ax blade or a hammerhead, for which he would whittle handles from nearby trees. In fact, he made whatever he could from what wood was standing around, so when it came time to install door latches and hinges on his log cabin, he devised an ingenious hinge mechanism with every part down to the dowel pins carved from heartwood.

Rory was so taken by Dick's ingenuity he embarked on carving a set of hinges for the fish house door, with an offer to do the same for the outhouse. Once the door was up and swinging, the hinges looked so impressive, Rory boasted up his handiwork with a lifetime guarantee.

Unfortunately, Rory hadn't noticed that in the film, the hinges were carved from blocks cut against the grain. The hinges held up until one day when I was standing just outside chatting with a neighbor. They split, and the heavy door came off and banged itself forward. I caught most of the weight on my wrists, where the skin was shorn so that afterward my dually bandaged wrists prompted meaningful looks from strangers who wouldn't have believed me anyway had I explained that a door walked into me.

Not that I would have held Rory to his guarantee; in the end, Jon and I thought it best to replace the hinges with wrought iron. The scars on my wrist are faded now, a bit like old cancellation stamps over a warranty.

I'd had in mind a quiet refuge in which to work, but the structure meant to be my studio quickly morphed into a kitchen. I do not have a room here but the woodland equivalent, a stump of one's own, where I've penned outhouse instructions and sappy potty haikus for its walls:

Real men pee outside
like hairy old Sasquatch does
Are you afraid to?

Lions and tigers
and bears and mice. Please cover
The toilet paper.

Please, nothing but pee
poo and TP down the hole
This loo does not flush.

Not that anyone spends more time in the outhouse than it takes to read three lines, since wolf spiders are great motivators to make haste, looking more like a wolf than a spider, burly, with hairy legs that can span a beer coaster. I confess I'm not very

Buddhist about the ones found in our sleeping quarters, and their aftermath is rather ghastly.

Each trip here requires the preparation of a camping trip. A few days before heading north, I'll fill square gallon jugs with water and set them in the freezer. Unlike blocks, bottled ice won't swamp the food as it melts, and once thawed, the bottles provide additional clean drinking water. Meals are planned in advance, a few cooked and frozen at home—usually soup, chili, or stew—to be eaten on whatever day it thaws. Fish or chicken for the grill is purchased frozen. Various batteries are plugged in to recharge. Duffels are packed with cabin clothes (extra socks, always). The ever-shuttling box of sheets and towels and bags of dry food are packed. Come departure day, the mail is stopped, the water turned off, electronics unplugged, plants doused. The car is jigsaw-jammed with coolers, water jugs, groceries, tools, guitar case, clean bedding, books, laptop, etc. On the road, there are the usual stops: Cloquet for gas and beer and a burger at Gordy's, Tower for bait and whatever additional groceries are needed. At this point, even the passenger's footwell is crowded with six-packs, food, or clear plastic bags delicately propped upright between feet, the minnows swimming in a silver funnel formation between ankles.

Upon arrival, we unpack the car, open the buildings, turn on the propane, carry water, dispose of vermin, shoo mouse turds from kitchen surfaces, wash counters, sweep dead moths and bugs from the floors, pitch the screen house, chant a blessing over the solar inverter, liberate bats, brush cobwebs and leaves from the outdoor kitchen, shake the spiders from the vinyl grill cover, then check to see if any have webbed over the gas jets (a potential propane tragedy), get a few casts in before dinner, hang the hammock, set up the camp chairs, gather wood, cook dinner, eat, boil water, wash dishes, break up kindling, build a fire, crack a beer, make the bed, fall into it.

More often than not, we're greeted with some unexpected challenge requiring a fix or solution, or two, or three. Last June, appropriately, every tall Juneberry bush along the road was pulled down by bears, making it impassable. In July, we found the exterior of the cabin riddled with splintered holes as if blasted by an M-80. Our first thoughts were vandals or nearsighted hunters. We squinted into the holes, stuck our fingers in, and examined the damage until a distant hammering sent palms to temples. A woodpecker, of course! It had been attacking the small wormholes in the timbers to get at the ants camped within. So an infestation as well, just our luck and the sort of dual setback that can devour days, requiring multiple trips to the hardware store. First there's chemical warfare waged against the pesky ants, then the wait for them to succumb, then filling the pecker-hole-anttombs with wood putty, then waiting for the putty to dry, then sanding, and finally staining the repaired holes to match the wood (not quite). Weekend kaput.

We've had more woodpecker damage over the years. After mulling over such deterrents as razor wire or steel siding, we discovered that things which flutter in the breeze will also keep the buggers from clinging and drilling. As a temporary solution, we tacked lengths of neon marking tape to the eaves like kite tails, and I made a mental list of things to find or make: beaded curtains, paper chains, grass skirts, Tyvek fringe, tinsel, bunting, feathers, Tibetan prayer flags, spoon chimes . . . Then I remembered the roll of yellow crime scene tape, much more appropriate. Yes, I finally admitted to Jon, renting *would* be easier and cheaper.

This is a potential workaholic's paradise. The toil can be all absorbing, which makes it doubly important to set aside time for leisure. And we do, to float aimlessly in the kayak, reading in the hammock strung between giant white pines at water's edge, sitting in the lounger cocked skyward to stare at the clouds, as good as blank pages.

Fifteen

People build in the middle of the woods for the peace and quiet. Here there is sometimes peace, but never quiet. In fact, the singular most surprising characteristic is the unceasing soundtrack that makes me think there really should be a name, like onomatopoeia, for a *place* that sounds like what it is.

The background choruses change by the hour, day, and season. Spring is a din of every bird auditioning at once. One mid-April dawn at the beginning of the avian mating frenzy, Jon and I were jolted upright in bed by a woodpecker announcing its territory, drumming the metal roof over our heads, loud as a Gatling gun.

There is usually a brief lowering of volume in April before the influx of summer birds when, as in *This Is Spinal Tap,* it goes up to eleven. Migrating species spotted at the feeders and birdbath out my office window in Minneapolis will usually arrive in the north about two weeks later. By June, the volume ramps so that you can barely hear the hummingbirds pip-thwitting overhead while trying to bat each other off the feeders. We'd hopefully hung red syrup feeders in the pines, unsure if this was too far north, but once filled, barely an hour passed before a squadron of ruby-throats blasted in as if shot from a cannon. Voracious, they were intent on draining every drop from the feeders, trying to guzzle their own weight—and rubies are good sized, as far as hummingbirds go. Once when Sam and I were in a nature preserve in Guatemala a tiny hummingbird took a liking to the bright band on my straw hat, and thinking it was an obscenely large bee, I swatted at it with the fervor of one about to be stung. An appalled onlooker caught my flippering hands and pointed out the creature was a *zunzuncito*, a little *buzz-buzz*, also known as the bee hummingbird; darling, once you know what they are. Their hardier northern cousins are twice their size and twice as bold. We watched from our lawn chairs as they dive-bombed the feeder, and Jon set his video camera on a tripod. We later slowed the speed to watch the comic action. With all their color and dash, the hummingbirds formed an airborne roller derby of Tinkerbells.

People are nearly reverent about the quiet here, the silence I have never heard. On summer nights, belchy frogs complain over the retorts of owls, owls are continuously interrupted by the batshitcrazy loons, and beavers applaud the loons with the sparest, most singular, and loud *claps* to the lake surface, reminding me of pre-lobotomy Jack Nicholson cheering on his bedlam of lunatics in *One Flew Over the Cuckoo's Nest*.

I'm a failure as a birder. I can look up a species five times in the field guides and by the next season forget which is what, who's who, or even that I'd seen a brown thrasher a dozen times before. I cannot keep bobwhite and bobolink straight, and while I know exactly what a white-throated sparrow sounds like, I could not pick one out if it landed on me. When we were children our mother could never keep our names straight, running through the entire roster of Mary-Valerie-Julianne before hitting *Sally!* My own memory is no better as I stand squinting skyward with arms akimbo, wondering, grosbeak? purple finch? redpoll? *house wren!*

In autumn, things settle. Seasonal birds haul south. Gray jays, also known as whiskey jacks, saunter down from the provinces to take over as the bad boys of winter. Here is the far southern border of the jacks' wintering range. *Here,* as far as whiskey jacks are concerned, is the equivalent of spring break at Daytona Beach with passes for free beer. Unlike their blue cousins, a jack's bullying actually exhibits some wit and trickery so that you can't help but like them.

Just passing through in October, rafts of cedar waxwings are often diverted from their migration to hang around awhile, even if just to clean up what shriveled Juneberries and chokecherries the bears didn't get. The waxwing is my favorite bird, its quiet trill as soothing as New Age flutes. The males and females have only slight variations in their plumage, androgynous in their Zorro masks and bodies feathered so finely they appear to be wearing teeny seal pelts. After I came across a freshly dead but seemingly uninjured male on the ground, I brought it inside and laid it out on a paper napkin. It weighed only about sixteen grams, the equivalent of two dark chocolate Dove Promises (the only available measure). I set the waxwing on the table and through the afternoon kept coming back to it to turn in it my palm, admiring and stroking the minute feathers, wishing for a magnifying glass and wondering how it had died. It was so perfect, not a scratch, with plumage a glistening caramel color like a licked Slo Poke. Its tiny bright yellow and bright red markings were mere ink dabs on its wingtips and tail feathers. I didn't want to give up the little corpse but then remembered the smell of perishable prizes I couldn't part with as a child—the rank shoebox holding a fish skeleton, a set of dead baby mice, the plaid cloth doll with the plastic mouth I force-fed with real milk.

After years of observing the bird feeder society, I've grown most partial to the underdogs, the little guys—wrens, finches, sparrows—and have concluded that of all avian society, robins are trailer trash: ungainly, creepy eyed, dimwitted, unwilling to share, too awkward to mingle. And homely—not even juvenile robins are cute. Oddly, our resident robin seem frightened of a little male goldfinch a fifth its size but bright as a Playtex glove, making me wonder if robins can detect alarming colors with their beady blank black eyes.

A rhythmic sewing machine sound led me through the woods to a tree with unmistakable markings: a sapsucker's signature holes, punch card neat and uniform as if made by machine, but by a bird that just sounds like one. In mid-October, most birds have flown off, just as whiskey jacks build their nests and settle in to harass and mimic the smallest mammals, doing a near-perfect chipmunk or squirrel, nattering right back at them even while stealing their stores. Balking crows fill in where the white-throated sparrow's song is memory, their call we were taught to remember by its mnemonic *kick your ass hee-hee, hee-hee*. To many, this bird's song is one that embodies north like no other. The few birds hardy enough to winter over here are tenacious: the crow, jay, and scrappy little chickadee, though they all clam up and listen when a hawk or eagle wheels overhead screaming for lunch.

What lulls exist—not silences, *never* silences—are welcome, especially in summer. I'm grateful for what is *not* heard—no traffic, no neighbor's too-loud *Best of ABBA* set on repeat, no lawn mowers or leaf blowers, no farting garbage trucks. Back in the city, such constant noises are layered against the freeway and air traffic, all topped by the drone of cicadas, which only gets louder as the days grow hotter, so electric sounding that as a child I assumed their angry buzz was the sound made by utility poles marked "Danger." After learning they were mere insects, I still thought of them as somehow dangerous; the only more awful-sounding bug would be a fly skidding around on its back in a skillet. The cicadas herald the dog days, the sweaty droop of summer and my least favorite time of year. It may well be that the *lack* of cicadas in the north is another lure that keeps me coming back.

In one of the camp recliners, perfect for stargazing or cloud watching, I can close my eyes and sounds surface: warm wind filtering through pine needles on scented huffs, a beaver tree groaning before its branches crash lakeward.

Water carries the minute noises so that while swaying in the shore-side hammock, I can make out the tiniest laps of water, a fish jumping, minnows going nuts in the bucket, curses of a neighbor across the lake trying to fix something.

When I think of summer, I hear it before I see it: breeze singing through metal porch screens, the clanking contents of a tackle box, a distant chain saw, a child cannonballing, the flap of a cribbage hand set down, thwacks of rolled magazines and the hiss of Raid, the *puhpuhpuh* of propane before ignition, tires on gravel, bedsprings whining, pee zizzing into an enamel chamber pot, the *fup* of a cap pried from a beer bottle, the five-horse death rattle of an Evinrude.

In winter, all sounds seem to contract so that you walk in a closed yoke of your own sounds: breath confined by parka hood, the fat *shish* of winter outer garments, the squeal of snow underfoot rising to castrato pitch as temperatures drop. Corn snow meeting window glass sounds like hurled grit, and chickadees that are only third-tier in summer become the nasal soloists of winter. On a deathly quiet night, you might hear a kill by a distant wolf pack, disturbed to discover that a deer can sound eerily human at the end. The *thuew-thuew* of lake ice cracking has an unearthly resonance that can be frightening when it occurs underfoot, signaling a change in temperature that actually strengthens the ice. Winter is a cold corridor of sounds.

Jon hears very little of the seasons. Since the surgery he'd had in his twenties to extract a tumor and the bat bones of his ruined eardrum, he's relied on his "good ear," which isn't all that good. More often I find myself refraining from asking, "Did you hear that?" I notice his increasing non-reaction to noises too high or thin to land in his range. Some decline seems inevitable and exhibits itself in small ways, like when he holds his guitar ever closer when tuning it.

I'd quietly subscribed to Internet sites that provide the latest information regarding advances in digital hearing aids, though getting Jon to wear his is like cajoling an overheated child into a snowsuit. I researched cochlear implants only to find they are roughly the price of real estate.

If anything good at all comes of his hearing loss, it's our routine of taking breaks twice a day to talk, face to face, either on the fish house bed or the loungers in the screen house with no distractions or radio. We catch up on the day, natter, make plans, joke around, debate, Jon reading more lip than he'll admit. This deliberate communication is our chance to give and get complete and focused attention, however brief. I would recommend such "sessions" to any couple, no impairment necessary.

He has already lost birdsong and whispers. I fear music and voices may be next, and there is no adapting for that. For Jon, it really *is* quiet here.

Sixteen

The same isolation that can render a community out of touch can also preserve its ethnic identities, not least those in the kitchen. Early on, even the smallest Range towns had established ethnic neighborhoods in which Italian, Finnish, Scandinavian, and Eastern European immigrants segregated themselves, bound among their own initially by language, later by choice, and often by food.

Though my family was Slovene, I'd heard older relatives refer to themselves as "Bohunks," and I grew up thinking we were Austrian, which was how many immigration ledgers listed incoming Europeans of the Austro-Hungarian Empire. For second- and third-generation Minnesotans, cultural differences and language barriers have long ago dissolved, but today people here still relate to their ethnicities and exhibit great pride in their heritages and can get very clannish about what goes into their sausages.

Food is the great unifier here, and culinary traditions run deep, often trumping taste. Booya and pierogi dinners are events, and Welsh pasty day means a run on the few bakeries left that make them. An entire diaspora of nostalgic Scandinavian Americans shares an inexplicable hankering for cod that's been salted, dried, and reconstituted by soaking in lye. Thankfully, lutefisk is only a seasonal Christmas staple, its yuck factor rivaling only Scottish haggis. In Norway, lutefisk is an export, has never been considered a delicacy, and is rarely, if ever, consumed. It might have been a necessary evil in the years before refrigeration, but no contemporary Norwegian chef would dry a perfectly good fish to the consistency of a salt lick and marinate it in dumpster juice.

Our Finnish Uncle Lew introduced us to *kalamojakka*—fish soup. *Mojakka* simply means stew, which, like "chowder," implies myriad variations. The proper pronunciation is "moy-uh-ka," though as kids we twisted it to "more-yukka." It can be delicious when made with salmon, cream, allspice, and chardonnay, but the version we knew was a thin soup of starchy potatoes and onions boiled in milk with northern pike, a fish considered too inferior and bony to eat as a filet. We ate with trepidation, lining up the translucent bones on the edges of our melamine bowls. A friend whose family eats mojakka at holidays reports that whichever of her siblings gets the fish head is still awarded a shiny quarter as compensation, though they are all over fifty.

Food is one topic on which most Rangers agree. I agree, for instance, that strudel is *good*, while head cheese is just a terrible lie. For one thing, there's no *cheese* involved; that's a diversion to trick you into eating it. And since there's no cheese, we are left to deduce that head cheese minus cheese equals . . . what? Imagine the contents of the slop bucket under a hog butcher's table: brains and cheeks, bits of snout, sinuses. Now imagine all that simmered and artfully arranged in a mold and then suspended in aspic (cook's decoupage), the result looking very much like a slice from the Body Worlds display at the science museum. I like to think those who actually serve the stuff shroud it with lettuce, actual cheese, and shields of bread to spare the victims. Blood sausage at least admits what it is.

A lot of this northern fare is home-cookin' comfort food but hardly healthy. Cholesterol-chocked dishes are staunchly defended as cultural badges, like Italian porchetta, the spiciest dish west of Wisconsin and east of the Dakotas and great on the grill, but off the calorie charts. Delicious locally made sausages and salamis are sodium torpedoes aimed at arteries. We loved Grandma Julia's pasties, malformed by her considerably quaking hands and made with pure lard pastry and generous pats of butter in the meat filling. When anything is "just like Grandma used to make it," the recipes should require a subheading by the Surgeon General. Everything Julia cooked got a chunk of butter tossed in at the beginning, the middle, and the end. Her walnut potica was mined with it, and heavenly. Julia would defend her butter habit as perfectly healthy, insisting it never killed anyone as vehemently as NRA supporters insist guns don't kill people. I'd watched her put butter in soup, and I've kept an eye on the kitchen sponge lest she butter that. Perhaps butter didn't do *her* any harm. She was never ill, and nearing a hundred, she was still trim with a heart like a Timex. I never saw anything like canned goods or mixes in her cupboards, and her kitchen garden was organic before the term implied righteousness. Everything was cooked from scratch, or *scratch*-scratch, as my friend Catherine calls any cake made with ingredients measured from canisters, while *single*-scratch is made from a box mix that you add eggs and oil to and bake, as opposed to the kind you add only water to before microwaving, which is just homemade.

Grandma's Parkinson's-like tremors prohibited her from drinking coffee from a cup. Instead she slurped from a saucer clamped in her quaking, translucent hands. A toddler in her lap might be in for a ride, but it could be disconcerting to walk into her kitchen when she was armed with so much as a paring knife or came swinging by like a bobblehead of herself carrying a saucepan of hot gravy.

For many years, I could not smell brewing coffee without thinking of waking up in Julia's house, nor could I pass a bakery without thinking of her cardamom braid, which was best either just out of the oven or six days later when it was rock hard and dipped in hot milk for breakfast—*buttered* hot milk.

Not everything around here is bad for you. An eat-locally gourmand might dream up a north woods feast that would include local fresh fish (a trout or sunny broiled up with sautéed morels), a wild watercress salad, and a blueberry tart on filbert crust—a meal that won't harm you. Alas, if you want fresh, you have to catch it yourself. The tourist favorite at restaurants is the walleye, caught in Canada, of course.

Here, a heart-smart meal might include local game, which is low in fat but particularly wild tasting since most mammals here survive on bark, twigs, moss, and what edible needles can be found. There's a reason hunters from downstate brag about bagging a corn-fed deer: the meat *is* better. The scraggly boreal diet of northern deer comes through in the venison, which tends to be waxy and tough, palatable only after long baths in red wine and many olive oil and garlic massages. Because of difficult logistics, deer are most often improperly dressed at the kill site—underdressed, actually. Ideally the animal should be immediately bled and skinned, then all fat cut away on-site. But more often, the carcass spends an hour or more thumping around in the back of a truck, which only infuses the skin oils and furry taste deeper into the meat. Once butchered, venison should be aged several days in cold water, rinsed countless times with fresh water, and plied with alcohol before a long simmer in some savory gravy.

Game birds are just as challenging. A meal of pheasant or grouse can mean chipping a tooth or cracking a crown on buckshot—hardly worth the risk. One solution is a product recently launched that lauds itself as "ammo with flavor," birdshot in cartridges packed with seasoned rock salt (in Cajun, lemon pepper, or garlic) that simply dissolves inside the bird's wounds. Just choose your flavor, load, and shoot.

It's a shame George Herter, Minnesota's own cranky hunter-poet-historian-chef isn't around to voice an opinion on Season Shot. Herter's *Bull Cook and Authentic Historical Recipes and Practices* was one of only two cookbooks in our mother's kitchen. The Betty Crocker was used as ballast and a doorstop, and Herter's was read for entertainment, though nothing much was prepared from it. These days there's a copy of Herter's on the cabin shelf and one in my kitchen at home. Having now read it from an adult's perspective, a cook's perspective, I appreciate its brilliance and oddness anew. I've yet to try many of the game recipes, like "Doves Wyatt Earp" (who knew he'd been a gunslinger *and* a gourmand?). It's easy to get sidetracked by all of Herter's asides, like how to survive an atom bomb attack or kill a wild boar with a shirt. A bull cook is one who works out of a lumber camp or fishing lodge, so by definition many of the recipes are simple and rustic, and given Herter's vast experience as an outdoorsman and chef, I trust his recipes are tried and true, though maybe not all his "facts" are. Did Genghis Khan really believe that after a raucous night of debauchery, the best way to restore mojo was by eating rhubarb? Much of Herter's wisdom is best consumed with a handful of salt, as is his self-help poetry or his marital advice book, *How to Live with a Bitch.*

As much as I'd like to try every recipe in *Bull Cook,* no water or refrigeration limits cabin cooking. At first we prepared food on either the one-burner propane camp stove or the rickety charcoal grill. The grill was eventually replaced by a larger propane model with a side burner, which meant we could heat water for dishes *while* making coffee or grilling toast—luxury.

Sam began barbequing in his teens, making easy things like Uncle Dave's mesquite stand-up chicken or Jamaican jerk. For his twenty-first birthday, he hosted a pig roast, procuring the pig and the mobile cooker and doing the whole thing himself. He's always been a good eater; his first words were food words, saying "more" before he could say "Momma." As a toddler, he would try anything from capers to Milk-Bones, and once on the dock at Rustic Resort, he nearly had the fishing lure that looked like a gummy worm to his mouth when I snatched it away. Meals could wholly occupy him, and when something was particularly good, his eyes glazed over. I discovered just how food-oriented Sam is as we leafed through a family photo album together and I pointed to an old vacation shot, lamenting that he'd been too young to remember the ferry ride we'd taken. He shrugged. "Teddy Grahams and applesauce with Rice Dream in my sippy cup." He'd been just over a year old. I flipped forward, testing him with a snapshot of him at two, holding a balloon. "Grandma Smith's birthday?" I posed. He shuddered. "Taco *casserole.*" I narrowed an eye, wondering if he remembered breast-feeding, hoping not.

Cooking outside is only fun until it starts to rain, or when the evening veil of mosquitoes descends just when your hands are slick with chicken blood, making it hard to defend yourself. The ultimate goal was to cook inside, but finding a gas range small enough to fit a hundred-square-foot kitchen was not easy. First I considered the old cast-iron, stand-alone footed cooktops with porcelain toggles, but they were never the right size, either two burners or four when three was my ideal. In any case, the safety factor eventually edged those out. I watched Craigslist for a twenty-inch apartment-sized gas stove to convert to propane. When the rare old stove did come up, it was usually advertised as "great for hunting shack," meaning it was chipped, filthy, or missing parts and burner tops. Still, the apartment stove seemed the best option, even if a bit large for the space. I'd followed the renaissance of midcentury appliances, entire businesses popping up to reclaim and restore them. The prices were a shock. Dealers' websites listed stoves like Granny's double-wide Hotpoint, spit-shined and newly chromed for five thousand dollars. I gazed longingly at pictures of appliances with dignified enamel insignias. O'Keefe & Merritt sounded like a vaudeville duo, and Roper Town & Country would have baked a thousand pies. The evocative Duparquet would never collapse a soufflé, a six-burner Western Holly would've rustled grub for a passel of farmhands, and the elegant Wedgewood on its curved legs looked as if it might cook only when it felt like it.

Back on Earth, my budget was two hundred dollars. I trolled Craigslist again, and patience eventually paid off when I came across a petite, freestanding, 1930s-era three-burner range that had sat rusting in a South Minneapolis basement since Prohibition. It was filthy but adorable on its little bowed legs, with an oven door that opened with a Bakelite knob. The top was a single molded piece of cast iron with simple star-shaped openings for burners. It was only 22 × 17 inches, and under the grime, the enamel was intact, a sort of pinky beige with cream and black accents. It would fit, was perfect, and I could afford it.

While researching how to remove rust and ancient grease, I discovered an old cook's trick for cleaning skillets. After gussying up in a respirator, goggles, and rubber gloves, I wrapped all the cast-iron parts in ammonia-soaked towels and stowed them in heavy plastic in a lidded galvanized trash can. Overnight, decades of baked-on gunk blistered and molted off like burnt skin. It worked swell on the burner top and dismantled innards, and a wire brush and steel wool got the rest. I rubbed stove blacking onto the cast-iron and gas tubes until they gleamed like licorice. A guy who fixed RV appliances swapped out the natural gas jets with brass propane versions and connections. With heat-resistant glossy enamel, I painted the squat little feet. All the while, women's names from the thirties sifted through my head. I wouldn't have consciously anthropomorphized a kitchen appliance and begun to think of her as "Mabel," but by then we had spent an awful lot of time together.

Mabel fits perfectly into the cabin but has proved a bit temperamental. She cooks awfully hot and might have been more aptly named Amber or Scarlett. Lighting a burner takes some finesse, but I've finally nailed the technique of whispering over her gas jets, ever so gently, blowing, "Please light, please, please light." If her cooktop is touchy, her oven is downright bitchy, and there's no telling what revenge Mabel might take on a batch of tater tots. The oven knob is on-off, with no temperature indicators or control. The lowest setting—meaning just enough flame so she doesn't sputter out and kill us by asphyxiation—averages around four hundred degrees. To bake anything all the way through requires rotating and shifting the pan from the top rack to the bottom rack halfway through and cracking the door a few times to lower the temp. Mabel has her good points, acting as an incidental furnace so that baking a coffee cake can heat the cabin for hours. Now we plan on charring cinnamon rolls or biscuits on cold mornings, scorching casseroles on chilly evenings, and baking nothing on warm summer days.

As my Aunt Mary used to insist, and as I try to convince Jon, charcoal in the diet is good for digestion.

Seventeen

If you're ever wondering if your guy is *the* guy, save yourself the gnashing and girlfriend advice and kill several birds with one stone and two plane tickets. Travel is the ultimate relationship hazing. You'll know within hours of landing whether he's finicky or easy, a control freak or able to roll with it, a wiener or a stand-up guy. If he pines for a burger when served an aromatic *tagine* or uses the phrase "these people" when referring to locals standing two feet away, ditch him in Fez. A man's travel persona is more revealing than his truck; only an autopsy says more. A trip is often the deal breaker.

Six months after we met, Jon and I embarked on the ultimate test and found cheap seats for the Bird Flu Tour of Southeast Asia, with an itinerary taking us to Thailand, Singapore, Hong Kong, and Bali, timed to coincide with a record heat wave and the impending avian flu pandemic.

Bangkok was shrill and hot. At each intersection was a belching rally of *tuk-tuks*, mopeds, and motorcycles with drivers yammering into cell phones and revving their engines, waiting for the green lights as if for checkered flags. The round window in our hotel room ran with condensation so that our view of the city was through a steamy porthole. Options for tourists were shopping, sex shows, or temples.

Hong Kong was gray, crowded, and fascinating. Singapore, just as hot as Bangkok, had an ash white sky and was oddly sterile and quiet—no surprise given that shouting, gum chewing, littering, begging, or public urination can land you in jail or get you publicly caned. Even the food in Singapore seemed timid, as if on its best behavior. In hundred-degree heat, we slogged along a sleepy, scorching beach and stumbled upon the start and endpoint of a triathlon. We watched as swimmers got out of the water to begin the run, the saltwater rivulets on their backs immediately turning to sweat. It was far too hot even to stand in the sun, let alone put one foot solidly ahead of the other.

Not the trip we'd dreamed of but awfully interesting, and by sheer luck, none of our eclectic group of tour mates was unbearable. We were looking forward to the last leg, a long stay in Bali on our own with no tour guide.

Normally just sweltering, Bali was so grossly humid even the locals were complaining and zombie-like. This was the heat of a prison laundry, surreal for anyone coming from a Minnesota February. Our pace was as fast as one can go while wading through knee-high porridge, our brains lightly simmering in our skulls. We lagged just behind ennui and lassitude, not even up for a debate on the precise differences between such words. We communicated like reptiles, blinking slowly at each other with about all the energy we could muster.

Curtains of humidity obscured the views from our beach hotel so that we never did see the much-touted vista of neighboring islands, or even much of the sea. It was too hot to wander anywhere on foot, so one day we hired a driver to take us up into the mountains, at least a few degrees cooler and where there were terraced rice paddies looking vaguely like those in the brochures, just visible through the murk. We got a slice of local culture when we came across a Balinese funeral cortège, no doubt for a victim of the heat.

Only our mornings had any form, and those could have occurred anywhere in Asia in any tourist hotel. We would linger over breakfast on a shaded veranda, bringing books and newspapers along to stretch out the meal, loath to leave a place with crushed ice and overhead fans, knowing that whatever was on our itinerary meant going outside, which meant a mixture of sunscreen and perspiration dripping into our eyes. Bali was a blur of various Holy and Important Sites, but we could hardly say we'd experienced the real Bali. Determined, we set out on our own with no plan, taking a taxi to nowhere with the idea of walking back. We lost track of where "back" was. The streets were so empty under the noonday sun that I realized the poem about mad dogs and Englishmen was a jab at all fools. Anyone sane was home napping. We eventually grew hungry but had spent our last *rupiah* on the taxi and couldn't find any cash machines because we were lost outside the tourist grid. We aimed and missed and aimed again in directions we hoped would lead us to our hotel. By then the heat oddly no longer warranted any mention, since 105 degrees and 96 percent humidity defied description, and complaining just took energy. We needed water. The only bright spot was that we didn't have to pee—didn't much need to anymore, all bodily fluids just sort of juiced out, wrung from our spongy limbs and places we did not know could sweat, like thumbs and elbows.

Bali is a spiritual place, and the kindly faces of its people reflect their Buddhist leanings and serene dispositions. So when we tried to take a shortcut through an outdoor market, we were shocked to discover that Balinese souvenir hawkers are maybe the most aggressive in touristdom. Deceptively delicate-looking females, aged prepubescent to crone, converged to shrilly and relentlessly badger us to buy pretty this for missy and pretty that for mister, following us and poking useless Chinese-made knick-knacks into our personal spaces.

We eventually escaped, made it back to our hotel, and collapsed.

I'd already planned for the evening to be special and made a reservation at a restaurant down the beach. After the day we'd just survived, we deserved it. Once the sun was safely down, I inched into my best dress, pinned up my limp hair, and poked on a pair of earrings. We snailed over to the restaurant for a romantic dinner with tables set out on the sand. Tiki torches lightly flickered in the breeze, waves lapped. Best of all, it was mercifully dark.

The mild breeze during wine and appetizers was welcome relief but turned less mild during salad and gained momentum over the main course, stilting conversation when gusts blew napkins or sand into our mouths. Waiters scurried, shoring things up and battening things down and apologizing as if the weather were their fault. Halfway through the seafood, the squall kicked up and fat raindrops drummed the table, prompting a hasty retreat to the dining palapa, though not quick enough to dodge the rain. Dinner had not been the romantic interlude I'd planned. When the rain let up, we bolted through the garden paths, Jon urging me onward through the downpour while the dots on my silk dress dissolved into a pattern resembling sperm. I urged him to slow down since hurrying wasn't going to get us there any drier, but just as I was about to ask him something important, he bolted again, digging for the room key.

After we dried off and fell into bed to wait for the AC to kick in, I could finally pose the question I'd been rehearsing during the long hours we'd been lost in the heat, the question bumping against my teeth throughout the clunky dinner, the one I'd nearly managed to gurgle out in the garden.

In one day, we had survived all the tests two people can when traveling in lockstep through all manner of exotic discomfort. And we were laughing about it. If we could make it through an afternoon like that, I figured we could face just about anything together. I thought back through my previous relationships— good and bad, long and short, happy and miserable—and through all the advice and warnings and commiserations friends and female relatives had offered in the years spanning my first bra to my first gray hair. Finally, for once, I no longer needed advice.

I nudged Jon. "Want to get married?"

〜

Along with happiness comes the rest of life—sometimes as a shit sandwich and sometimes in letter form.

Dear Ms. Stonich,

As you are likely aware, Minnesota Department of Transportation is in the process of developing a major road project that may result in realigning and reconstructing Highway 169 between S_____ Road and C_____ Road . . .

The rest of the letter, bureaucratic glossolalia worded to sound benign, translated roughly to "a road directly through the middle of the highest elevation of your most beautiful acres, which we will be seizing, blasting, bulldozing, and realigning, effectively destroying the market value of your land as well as any sentimental value it might have to you or your loved ones."

Each word felt like a punch. This was our first official communication from Mn/DOT, even though they and the local task force had been planning this reroute for nearly a decade—close to the number of years I'd been toiling to build and improve our little haven, all the while clueless that the work and time and investment could amount to nothing. The letter closed by saying that come spring, a bulldozer and drilling rig would arrive to crisscross the property to gather mineral samples and tear up the terrain.

At first, no one believed the proposed plan would actually go forward because a child could see it was too illogical. The $22 million budget was intended to improve all fifty miles between Highway 53 and Winton, a few miles east of Ely. But according to this plan, they would blow their entire wad on four miles. I kept asking the question "Who would reroute a four-mile stretch that is statistically less dangerous than the other forty-six?" I kept getting the same answer—*a state agency.*

When I asked Mn/DOT why we hadn't been contacted sooner, I was told by the project manager that the agency is under no legal obligation to notify or enlighten affected homeowners beyond posting a small notice in the local paper. You've seen these notices, usually at the bottom of the classifieds, in infinitesimal type requiring Mr. Magoo goggles to read.

I'd spent years finding the place, and for eight more I'd worked like an illegal to make the raw land habitable and navigable, building what shelters I could. I'd been lucky enough to find a willing partner to share a future with, and just as we had begun to entertain visions of spending our retirement here, our golden years, we discovered the state had other plans for us, that they have the right of eminent domain and we have jack.

The current highway as it sits is two-thirds of a mile away from the cabin as the crow flies and on the opposite side of a steep ridge of state land that abuts ours. Between here and there are two more high ridges and valleys that muffle highway noise as effectively as waffle foam. To actually *see* the road, one must hike a rough half hour over our back acres. The line drawn for the new highway cuts close to the cabin, smack on top of the nearest ridge, the very beautiful ridge we would like someday to build a hermitage on, perfect for its isolation and amazing view. The road would bisect the ridge, cutting us off from an undetermined number of our acres. Worst of all, we'd experience wave after wave of noise from traffic that could even be close enough for us to *see*.

Dreams of sitting on our lovely ridge at sunset morphed into nightmares of a paved speedway with trucks barreling over, growling to downshift. It became impossible to lie in bed without anticipating a future throbbing with the roar of a murder of Harleys and diesel-powered semis. My overwrought imagination conjured the din of a truck pull.

Cabin life suddenly became less than: less than enjoyable, less than hopeful. It was difficult to rouse enthusiasm for the future or find motivation to keep improving the place. Should we cut our losses and sell?

When I broached the subject with Sam, he balked without a tic of hesitation. "No!"

We found out what we could: what avenues we might take, what recourse we might have, what the odds might be. Mostly we sit in stasis, writing editorials, sending letter after letter to state officials and environmental groups, local politicians, and any organization that, like us, might want better answers from Mn/DOT.

It's long been the local convention that anything bringing money and jobs to the area is sacrosanct, and anyone who questions the means is the enemy. Even locals who think the reroute is ill planned shrug and relent, the general attitude being that you cannot fight what Mn/DOT has wrought, in the same way you cannot take on big mines or big industry. Things have always been this way, and anyone naïve enough to think otherwise is in for a load of heartache.

Some days it seems easier to give it all up rather than go through the anxiety, to just let the ax fall and bulldozers bull. Jon, more rational, suggests we might wait to see just how bad it will be. But I *know* how bad it will be, and I'll prepare for battle with everything I have: nothing. It seems inconceivable that our land might become a long ditch, our buildings sold or hauled away, that our picnic site will become a gravel pit. Such possibilities go down like swallowing burrs. Still, we must start considering the worst, that our time here might come to a premature end. And delving deeper into that possibility and getting a little existential, I have to admit that we don't matter to the land in the way the land matters to us, despite our feelings of stewardship or how long we are here. Whether it's ten years or sixty, we are only passing through.

⌒

During the last four years of this ever-looming threat, there have been brighter moments in life. A year after we met, Jon and I returned to the courtyard restaurant where I'd first gazed upon his dimples. This time with fifty or so friends and relatives, I looked up at my groom.

If I had to compare, I'd say he is a cross between Dudley Do-Right and Jon Stewart, loyal and steadfast, smart and irreverent. Like Stewart, Jon is funny enough to make me nearly pee my pants and handsome enough to make me want to take them off. Like Dudley, he leads with a brave chin and is largely unaware of his own charms. I know that if I were lashed to railroad tracks, he'd be to the rescue in a flash, offering to tie me up someplace more comfortable.

"I *do*," I said. Then shouted it just to make sure he could hear me.

Eighteen

FURNISHED LAKESHORE CABIN. THREE ACRES ON GOOD WALLEYE LAKE. NINETY-NINE YEAR LEASE AND BOAT INCLUDED (LEAKS). TWO-SEATER OUTHOUSE. $1,000.00

In 1963, a thousand dollars could buy a cabin. Still, it was a major expense given Dad's income, but maybe he overextended himself knowing it would vex our mother, who visited the cabin just once, all the while complaining about the bugginess, the dampness, and the outhouse, mincing around as if there might be teeth in the grass. The rest of the time, she sat in the sun with a beer and the transistor radio, an ashtray balanced on the middle stripe of her swimsuit. When bored, she tempted us closer to her lawn chair with peanuts, then clamped us between her knees and riffled our scalps looking for ticks, drawing hard on her cigarette when she found one, searing them with the lit end so that while we were tick free, we stank of burnt hair and sometimes had little oozing blisters where she'd missed.

After the divorce, Dad rented a mobile home in a creepy trailer park in town. It had a plaid banquette that folded out into a lumpy bed where we slept when visiting, but with the cabin, he had a real place to bring us on weekends. Despite its lack of electricity and running water, it was a huge improvement over the trailer.

Mother never came to the cabin again, and on ensuing Friday nights, while she was sausaging herself into a girdle and applying orange lipstick before heading down the street to Big Stan's Tavern, we waited on the porch for Dad's honk. Before the Rambler rolled to a stop, we had its doors open and were piling in with our grocery bags of clothes and pillows.

Fifteen miles out of town, we stopped at the bait shop, where we cruised the rows of aerated tanks full of crappie minnows, fatheads, shiners, chubs, and spottails. The tubs hissed and bubbled, and the minnows swam circles like vortexes of beer can tabs. I stared at the chubs, imagining what sort of monster could swallow one. Surely a fish large enough to eat a chub could be tempted by a swimming child's toe.

Once the frantic minnows were scooped into the holey metal bucket-within-a-bucket, Dad wedged it behind the driver's seat to stay upright so that for the duration of the drive it sloshed a fishy smell and splashed our shins at the worst bumps. The styrofoam containers of leeches and worms were so repulsive we didn't even toy with their potential since dangling one at a sibling would mean touching one. The leech carton went on the shelf behind the backseat, where we could keep an eye on it now and then during the long ride.

If nobody had vomited by the midway point, we stopped for ice cream. Just past the drive-in, there was a lake with a bridge where people fished standing or from folding chairs, having no boats or cabins of their own. Dad never failed to "ho-ho" every time we passed them, with a smug "Guess we know where the poor people are fishing tonight!"

Not like our place was all that. No cars passed by on our narrow dirt road, but if they did, the drivers would probably smirk, "Guess we know where the people with crappy cabins are sleeping tonight!"

Cramped and damp as it was, the cabin was in a lovely setting, on a deep, non-weedy lake, with few neighbors. It was dark and smelled like mice, but we didn't spend that much time inside, anyway. Mostly we were in the boat, on the dock, in the water, or on the spit of land that stuck out like a tongue as if the opposite shore were a sister. On the spit was a fire ring and circle of lawn chairs that made a safe zone of firelight when the night crept up from behind.

Friday night at The Lake was pizza night. As soon as we arrived, Dad mixed up the dough from a Chef Boyardee box and set it to rise. While it was still light outside, he'd go hang the motor on the boat, turn on the propane, mow the few tufts of grass, or dispose of dead vermin. We cut little rounds of hot dog for pizza topping and battled over who would open the can of sauce, who would pour the sauce over the dough, who would arrange the hot dog rounds, nearly coming to blows over who would open and sprinkle the cheese packet.

With pizza, we each got a little glass of beer. At home, we even had our own tiny steins from our dead grandmother's china cabinet. My stein was long gone, broken after I'd been refused service. Over my limit of four ounces and incensed, I'm told I'd hurled my empty stein at the wall opposite my high chair. At the cabin, we drank from little Grain Belt glasses with red diamond logos.

We were taught to light the propane lamps with caution so as not to blow up the cabin or ourselves and warned not to poke matches up into the expensive mantles. The mantles were silk, burned to white ash and delicate as lace, making it nearly impossible *not* to poke at them, just to see what would happen. The wooden match had to be lit and ready at the precise second the gas knob was turned and hissing. Any delay and too much gas made a loud *ploop* and a mini explosion inside the glass globe. A match held too close to a mantle without enough gas would scorch it. Always there was the scary *puh puh puh* of pulsing gas and the threat of singed eyebrows. We stood on the table to light the big double globe as night turned the cabin windows into black mirrors. Only when all the mantles were lit and settled like blazing moon drops could we relax.

After supper, frogs cranked to compete with the radio and the staticky stations from Ontario. We played poker on the heavy dining table with the linoleum top, its ornate varnished knees banging ours. Dad dealt cards while lying to us, insisting that he knew Sheriff Matt Dillon and that we were part Indian, making us shrug at each other's pale towheadedness.

Even though the darkness outside seemed something alive to stumble through, come bedtime it was preferable to brave it, along with a short row over black water to the island to sleep in the tent rather than the boxy little cabin bedroom with its rickety aluminum bunks and tiny window and Dad snoring like a mower just a chipboard wall away.

On the big island, Dad had cleared a space and built a platform on which he set up a roomy green army tent. The tent had screened windows with roll-down shades and a wide door flap that was roped to the trees, making a little covered porch. It was big enough for real beds, a dresser, and our own kerosene lamp. On sunny mornings, the air inside was olive hued, the branches and leaves outside scrawling their shapes on the walls. On a rainy day, there was no better place to curl up with a volume of condensed books, hopefully one with a mystery or near-death cliffhanger. When rain thwapped overhead, the smell of wet canvas grew musty, pages rippled, and plots thickened.

Over the decades since, I would think back to reading in that tent whenever I found a new addition for my haphazard cabin library (now in boxes in the Mayflower trailer) of stories chosen for summer reading. The library includes the adventure classics I'd always meant to read, like *The Last of the Mohicans, Heart of Darkness, White Fang, Moby-Dick, Kidnapped, The Red Badge of Courage, The Red Pony,* and the girl books I intend to reread: *Anne of Green Gables, Kristin Lavransdatter, Little Women,* and all of Jane Austen. There are books specific to the region, some recently reread, like the Sig Olson books and my freshly scored first editions of Helen Hoover. There's a pile of field guides and natural history books: *Ferns of Minnesota, Mosses and Lichens, Trees of North America, Woodland Flowers of the North,* a half-dozen bird guides, how-to books on log building and stone building, vintage cabin plans, and stacks of *National Geographic* magazines so old they don't have pictures on the front, only contents.

There's an abundance of the book genre my sister Valerie and I shared an appetite for as kids: true stories of near-death experiences and tales of survival and deprivation—accounts of people folded into avalanches, mauled by rogue animals, adrift in dinghies and surviving by drinking puddle water or their own pee, shivering under a fuselage lean-to they'd built with their one remaining arm. We speed-read books with the specter of death looming, scrabbling over pages to reach the brink. True crime books were usually on a reserve list but worth the wait; a wacko slow roasting his victim or stitching one to a tree could make a bullying boy or vicious nun seem nearly pleasant by comparison. My middle-school vocabulary expanded to include such words as "vivisection" and "flense."

Eager for stories of childhoods more grim than our own, we devoured books that made life in Proctor, Minnesota, seem like a romp despite our proximity to the rail yards, or that mother sold food stamps for cash, or that our parish priest was a repeat offender pedophile. The town library had a few dusty volumes of Dickens, whose descriptions of hovels and chilblains made our box of a house feel downright cozy. Drafts that lashed at ankle height didn't seem so bad after reading about Victorian cold-water slum flats with only smoky coal fires for heat and reeking privies for toilets. Being banished to our rooms had nothing over Little Dorrit, born in a debtors' prison. Accounts of hunger made our mother's meals (fried bricks of hamburger and boiled bricks of frozen vegetables glued together over stretchers of tepid boiled potatoes) seem feastly.

I sought stories representing the polar opposite of whatever the current season or situation was. Hot nights at the lake were made more tolerable by reading about Arctic and Antarctic exploration, a sort of hyper-deprivation genre featuring the likes of Thierry, Amundsen, or Shackleton trekking to places where chances were, if you did survive, you might leave behind bits of your face. My favorite cooling-off books were *The White Dawn,*

Kabloona, and the prize for the you-think-you've-got-it-tough Arctic chronicle, *Book of the Eskimos.* For cold nights there were *The Jungle Book, Kim, Kon-Tiki,* and dog-eared Westerns.

The old cookbooks are crammed in with the collection: *Herter's,* of course, but also *Campfire Girls Cook!* and *One Pot Meals,* with recipes like Mushers Mash and other meals that could only taste good eaten outside by famished campers. Together, the collection comprises a library meant to be read in aluminum lawn chairs, porch swings, and hammocks.

On nights Sam and I played Cabin!, we would tuck in with Jack London or Bret Harte, and when Sam grew droopy, we'd end with something more upbeat so that the sometimes tense plots didn't trail into his dreams. He loved bits of *Hiawatha's Childhood,* so I tried to keep up Longfellow's over-the-top singsong cadence: "Wah-wah-taysee, little firefly, little flitting white-fire insect, little dancing white-fire creature, light me with your little candle, ere upon my bed I lay me, ere in sleep I close my eyelids." By the time I'd gotten to "little candle," he'd be out himself, like a thwapped bug.

Outside the green tent were green woods and more woods, with countless crannies and solitary niches and alcoves to explore. Half a mile away behind an old hunting shack was a bog and a deep glade that smelled of church incense, the spongy earth hosting a neat copse of cedar, some trunks so curved they made shapes like pipes under a sink. The best spot was a piney corridor that led to the hobbity hollowed trunk of a great burnt pine, big enough to stand in. Not far was a creek as narrow as a run of Glad Wrap and bridged by a corduroy path of cedar logs. Close to the cabin was a place I visited most often, a birch grove with a peculiar double-humped rock that fit my bottom as if I'd sat down just as the lava was cooling.

The Lake hadn't always been a lake. It had once been a river valley with houses and old farms, and Dad said maybe even Indian camps. But the power company needed a dam, so the trees were logged out, the buildings abandoned, and the valley flooded. Intrigued by the idea there'd once been people living just under where we fished, I constantly hung over the bow of the boat, squinting in hopes of seeing remnants—a chimney, a windmill, a silo—but the lake water was tinted and clouded with iron and gave up nothing. I could only imagine people coming and going between their underwater teepees, farming their underwater farms. I supposed they climbed the islands that were once hills in their landscapes, but as thoroughly as I combed them hoping for an arrowhead or old tool or bottle, I never found so much as a rusty nail.

This is where Dad brought us. It was somewhere good. Parents couldn't always be relied on, but the hollow tree would always take me in, saying just the right thing—nothing. This place wasn't going anywhere. It wasn't going to disappear or frighten or worry me, and during the long squall that was our parents' divorce, it was sometimes the best and only harbor.

After Dad died, the cabin stood neglected for years, barely used. I rarely visited, and the older I got, the smaller and grubbier it seemed. After a time it didn't even have beds; the fridge was hauled away; the well dried up. The tent collapsed onto its platform, and the platform collapsed into compost.

Dad's will stipulated that the cabin and lease could not be sold unless all of us kids agreed, knowing that since we'd never agreed on anything, chances were it would stay in the family. Half my siblings walked away from it. I hung on to my share out of nostalgia, eventually selling it to my sister Mary. The little cabin is gone now, but before it was torn down, the pine paneling was salvaged to make kitchen cabinets for the new cabin, a three-bedroom, two-bath summer home with a laundry room and heated floors. Mary stripped the heavy dining table we learned to play poker on, and the junky thing we'd never really noticed turned into a glossy antique.

Dad's fishing hat hangs in roughly the same spot by the door, and nearby is a framed photo of him holding a stringer heavy with at least a dozen fish, captioned "Matt with six walleyes" (the legal limit). The new porch overlooks the cement slab of the old cabin, now only a shape.

Nineteen

Julia Stonich died in the summer of 1987, just before Ely celebrated its centennial. Had she hung on a few months, she'd have turned one hundred along with the town and been coiffed and powdered and propped up to ride in a float. Maybe anticipating that parade she may have intended her final nap be intentionally deep.

At the funeral, I was many months pregnant with Sam. As if by some feat of synchronized ovulation, two of my sisters were also pregnant, all of us due to give birth within weeks of each other.

I don't remember the service, only the gathering in the church basement, a sticky July affair made more humid by gallons of boiling coffee. Sandwich loaves frosted with cream cheese swagged in the heat while the windows wept, and my sisters and I tucked bits of food into our purses. I drove back to Grandma's house, a signature old-lady white two-story clapboard with dark green trim and lace and violets at the windows. Walking in, I wasn't terribly sad. Julia had simply finished with a long life while I had an impending lapful of it pressing my ribs and boxing my bladder. Life, at least the cyclical aspect, was starting to make sad sense. Since I was no longer a daughter or granddaughter to anyone, it seemed appropriate I was about to become someone's mother.

I stood at the sink and looked out Julia's window to the brick building next door where the spinster Janko sisters had lived since time immemorial. The first floor housed their beauty parlor, with Garbo-vintage perm machines that looked like they could get you to confess anything. The salon walls were covered with faded posters of women with Joan Crawford waves, their once–bright red lips faded into pairs of bloodless slugs. As kind as the Jankos had been to our grandmother over the years, we didn't want them anywhere near our hair.

Dad told a tall tale about the sisters both being in love with the same soldier who died in a war (he didn't say which war, and looking at the sisters, you couldn't imagine). This was a common enough story, which Dad then made ridiculous by adding that after the body was returned home for military burial, the sisters waited a proper few years before digging him up, when they split the pile of bones in a macabre one-for-you, one-for-me divvy wherein each got a hand, foot, femur, ribs, toe bones. Splitting his skull wasn't an option, so they took turns, a week on, a week off. This was around 1967 when *Psycho* was finally going to be aired on television. Since our mother thought us too impressionable to watch it (she'd obviously never checked our stacks of library books), Dad must've felt compelled to supply his own dose of horror. Eventually the sisters began bickering over the skull so bitterly that one night the skeleton had had enough of their hair-splitting and hitched itself back together, grabbed its own skull, and huffed off in the direction of the cemetery, where it buried itself and finally got a decent night's sleep.

The sisters then went back to being just the old ladies we knew. Of course, not much of anything ever happened to the

Janko sisters, though they did go on to invent the Ely Bikini, which consisted of a red railroad kerchief and two safety pins. The kerchief was tucked into the bottom of a bra, and the top corners were pinned onto each strap. From behind, the Ely Bikini looked just like what it was, a grungy brassiere, and since "the girls" only ever donned these costumes to garden, they were usually bent over anyway, looking just like two biddies weeding in their underwear.

~

The rooms in Julia's house were neat pods. She'd accomplished an admirable feat at her very advanced age, to live clutter-free. Her spare house contained a bit of furniture, a few watercolors and oils painted by my aunts, and remarkably few other possessions for someone nearing one hundred. Still, the house had never felt bare until that afternoon. The silence echoed: no Julia mumbling back at the radio, no slurp of tea from saucers held by hands too shaky to hold cups, no squawk from the kitchen announcing supper, no more rogue farts preceded by her warning, "Eruption!"

She'd been a great cook of simple cuisine. Her chicken paprika and warm potica were all the more appreciated when compared to our mother's wild stabs in the kitchen. Staring into Julia's fridge, emptied save a can of ARCO coffee and a box of baking soda, I said a silent good-bye to her strudel, her milky coffee, and the cider-vinegar dressing she made to splash over fresh lettuce and onions still warm from her garden.

Julia's punctured-tire voice and manner of speech might've been called wise-croaking. She'd been agile minded and witty, as were her children. I did not understand until I was old enough to have spent time with other families that not everyone appreciated irony, that not all family gatherings crackled with sarcasm, that not everyone was comfortable with jabs or got the joke.

Julia had been the very last of her generation, had outlived her siblings, husband, and all but one of her sons. Then she slipped off the log like the frog in the song, her spot about to be filled with the baby I was not so much carrying as lugging and the two babies my sisters were about to drop. And while it might have appeared that our family baby boom was planned, it was accidental; fitting though, that there would be three new beings to replace Julia, who in spite of her size had been a big presence.

I vividly recalled being about seven or eight and sitting at the dinner table while she drank coffee from her deep china saucer. At some point during dessert, I made some wrong move, and my plate back flipped into my lap. I immediately burst into tears, sure I would be punished. The only shorts I had with me were ruined, splotched purple—and worse, I'd lost my dessert to the linoleum. But Dad and Grandma acted like it was nothing. They merely righted me, dabbed my tears, and gave me a fresh dish of blueberry cobbler. This had been a safe house, where being a child was forgivable.

I stepped outside to the kitchen garden, where Julia had grown what few vegetables thrive here: lettuce, stunted carrots, and green onions. Along the fence, the grapevines Joe once harvested for wine had shriveled. There were still a few volunteer clumps of chives and horseradish creeping to take over, the edges frilled with weeds. I wanted badly to kneel and pull them, knowing Julia wouldn't have liked the untidiness, but I feared I wouldn't be able to hoist myself back to standing. So I pulled what I could, supporting myself on the pickets as I went, needing to do this one last thing.

After I wedged in behind the wheel and began driving away, scenes escorted me out of town. I recalled watching television with Grandma when I was a teen and an ad for feminine deodorant came on. She threw her hands in the air, croaking, "Jesus God in Heaven, what'll be next, nut spray?!" In the early seventies, when I showed up with my blond hair chemically sprung into an Afro, she barely looked up from the crossword, her one dry comment being, "So, you're a Negro now?"

One day when I was about seventeen, Dad and I were turning over her garden, and seeing that we were working up thirsts, Julia went out to buy beer. Not wanting to be recognized going into the liquor store at high noon, she'd put on a head scarf and sunglasses—forget that she'd lived in Ely fifty years and every soul knew her pigeon-toed shuffle at fifty yards.

Not long after that, when I was too busy to go along with him to visit Grandma or go to the cabin, Dad began complaining, which wasn't like him. At first I thought he was just annoyed because he wanted a driver, great road-napper that he was. He'd wanted to take my little niece north one weekend when I wasn't available, having promised to help a friend move out of town. He canceled the trip altogether, getting huffy.

"What?" I asked, to no response. I was eighteen, had a job, friends, a social life. What did he expect? On the Saturday morning after helping my friend, I woke up confused, halfway across the state on a strange couch. Suddenly, inexplicably, I needed desperately to go home. I drove as fast as I could.

The house was empty, and when someone with a key came in, I assumed it was Dad, but it was one of my sisters with the news. I sat down hard and Margaret jumped in my lap. She was very much Dad's pet by then and spoiled rotten despite his alleged disdain for the species.

I kneaded Margaret's ruff a little too hard as my sister explained (as if one can), but after the first sentence with the unfathomable words in it, I didn't take in much more and just watched her mouth make shapes. This wasn't how it was supposed to happen. My father wasn't supposed to die at a rummage sale while buying a boat (though much later I would think, well, he *did* enjoy a good rummage sale and was awfully fond of boats).

He'd known he wasn't well. His heart problem was the same genetic glitch he'd already lost three brothers to, a valve malfunction that these days could be diagnosed in a routine doctor's visit and fixed using things from a sewing kit.

Indeed, he had flaws beyond the physical. He'd been a bit of a cheapskate, which was forgivable since he'd lived through the Depression and never had a really well-paying job. He had some racist notions that he'd kept to himself until confronting me once for having danced with a black boy, when I got the "not with my daughter" speech. And it was probably best he never much drank because he couldn't hold his liquor, one example being a Christmas several years after the divorce. Mother was bent over, clearing the post-gift-opening frenzy of wrapping paper and packaging. Dad was seated just behind her, perfectly situated, and, being in his cups, was unable to resist planting a foot on his ex-wife's bottom and toppling her headlong into the Christmas mess.

He *was* awfully good to his mother, though.

I still wonder what it must have been like for my grandmother to see four of her five sons die. I couldn't imagine it, and perhaps my aunts couldn't either, so to protect her, they kept the news of Dad's death from her for as long as they could, none eager to be the one to tell her that Matt was gone.

Now they were both gone. Just outside of town, I pulled over to blot my eyes. When I finally looked up, I realized I'd stopped in front of the Mad Pruner's house. The low yellow ranch house was the landmark that let us know we were almost there, almost to Ely. The house was nearly swallowed from behind by boreal forest, but the front yard was a half acre of manicured lawn with evergreens trimmed into tight topiary, neat as trees glued in a model railroad landscape. The conical spruce and balsams were clipped with precision and stood like sentinels, as if to keep the wilderness at bay, a civilized front daring the wilderness to encroach any further, daring time to march on.

But it does, and the name Stonich has grown scarce. The family history is here, but no family. I was reminded of Edward Gorey's book *The Dwindling Party,* in which members of a Victorian picnic wander off one by one to go wading, hiking, and bird-watching, and one by one they do not return (drowned, plucked up by birds, conked). *We* dwindle, our name cropping up more often on headstones than in phone books. Across the Range are only a few uncles twice removed and murky third and fourth cousins unknown. As I drove away from Ely, it occurred to me that a whole branch of the family tree had just snapped. Julia had been the youngest of her siblings, the very last of her line. Her children had either trickled away or died. Driving south, I wasn't certain *I* would ever be back. At the conclusion of *The Dwindling Party,* the one dazed survivor walks off on the last page. Just like that.

Twenty

If we walk a mile in any direction from the cabin, we know every neighbor we encounter. That's only about a dozen or so people, but on our city block in Minneapolis, I know maybe two souls, and Jon, who's lived here twenty years longer, knows only a few more. At The Lake, we are more involved neighbors by choice. We're all in it together, mostly.

The Allens had the whole lake to themselves until a dozen years ago, when surrounding land was sectioned into parcels by U.S. Steel and sold, and new landowners (us) converged. They've taken the intrusion quite graciously. If The Lake had a mayor, Larry would be it: steady on and unflappable, definitely unmovable, and, being here the longest, the most knowledgeable about the place. If Larry doesn't have the answer to some question, he knows someone who does. We met the day Terry and Susan and I first trudged The Lake looking for the land, a freezing February afternoon spent veering on and off the snowy road searching for the property, getting loster and colder by the minute. We finally found the shore; identified our parcel; declared, "Yup, this will do"; and turned back to tromp to the car a mile away on feet that felt like anvils. We barely got going when we strayed down a spur, thinking it would lead us to the main road. We knew we were lost again when we came across a cabin, a truck, and Larry.

Larry apparently assumed we were all female. Terry wore his wavy hair long in those days, and between looking coiffed and his stature, he was often mistaken for a homely ma'am. Susan is so petite my former brother-in-law pronounced her the "goddamndest smallest full-growed woman" he'd ever seen and also cautioned the couple against wearing blue or they'd be mistaken for a pair of Smurfs.

Jacketless in the single-digit weather, Larry was taking a beer break from whatever chore he'd been at when we interrupted. He was about the goddamnedest biggest full-growed man *we'd* ever seen, particularly when planted next to Susan. Holding up his can of Bud (the size of a cork in his mitt), he offered us girls a beer, which we only declined because it wasn't hot. Gathered into his windbreak, we pummeled Larry with questions about The Lake, the area, other neighbors. We were a bit overexcited about the land and jittery with cold, and Terry was coming down with some flu, so we were grateful for Larry's offer to drive us back to our car. Dropping us off and backing away, he waved, probably relieved, maybe hoping he'd seen the last of us.

He hadn't. Not long after the snow melted and we finally had the deed to the land and were bona fide neighbors, I was driving the muddy road and got stuck after swerving from one bad dip into a worse one. My cell had no reception to call AAA. When I stopped cursing and whimpering, I could hear a far telltale buzzing, either a chain saw or a wood chipper, someone nearby either stocking their woodpile or getting rid of evidence. I honked a distress honk, and soon Larry pulled up with his son, Garth, who is even bigger, each arm the size of a toddler.

Larry and Garth gingerly hooked up my bumper, sturdy as a pie tin, and blinked in stony amusement at my headlights, each with its own mini wiper. They had the car unstuck in a minute, and once the chains were dropped and the car was rolling, Larry called out, "Don't stop," by which he likely meant, "Please, God, don't let her stop."

A few summers later on a hot, windy day, Larry was driving with Garth on the old logging road and for no good reason turned down our driveway, which was odd since Larry's not the drop-in-on-a-whim sort. At the end of the drive, he could see the cabin was nearly built, and nearly set to burn down. Either Rory or Lars had failed to extinguish a fire in the pit, and it had smoldered its way underground along the roots of a small pine growing smack next to the cabin deck. Larry and Garth commenced putting out the fire with what was available: scraps of slab wood, the heels of their Paul Bunyan boots, and a five-gallon bucket of logger's caulk. Larry left a note on the only thing around to write on, the back of a FLAMMABLE! sign, scrawling a sooty "Watch your fires!" It was months before we discovered it had been Larry who'd saved the cabin. He hadn't signed his note, almost as if he didn't want word of his favor getting back to us.

Directly across the lake are Derek and Amy. Both lived in major cities before moving here, where they now dedicate themselves to a north woods aesthetic with the keenness of reenactors. When not crafting birch-bark canoes, Derek builds small, charming timber-frame cabins called WeeCabins. His outhouse model is listed in the brochure as the WeeWee. Several of these structures have been commissioned by neighbors so that his alpiney chalets dot the lake like so many cuckoo clocks and cuckoo crappers. On high occasions, Derek dresses like a voyageur in blouse and sash with his long braid beribboned. For weekday casual, he dons a sort of Depression-era twee of henley shirts, red suspenders, and high lace boots, looking just like a CCC recruitment poster.

Some neighbors we see only a few times a season. The Blaines are from out of state, a plastic surgeon–poet and his southern belle wife. As owners of one of only two wells on the lake, they are generous with their water, leaving their hose out for us dry beggars.

Paulie and Lana are the resident foodies. Paulie's a New York Italian who likes nothing more than to fuss and feed people, and Lana is his intrepid *sous-chef*/bottle washer. They regularly manage multiple-course feasts with no running water, a dorm fridge, and a gas stove the size of an Easy-Bake oven. Every autumn when Paulie cooks for a group of hunters, I like to assume he wears a blaze-orange apron.

Mac and Lu might be called the Sensibles. Mac is a bespectacled geologist seemingly in a constant state of rumination. He built their log cabin himself, no easy feat given the size of the logs, and when we scratch our heads trying to figure out *how*, we all take on Mac's look of concentration. Lu, a nurse who's seen it all, seems calmly at the ready to catch something in midair or stitch someone up. Mac's current mission is to prove our ridge is too environmentally precarious to handle the proposed highway reroute. To that end, he roams the woods with a pickax, trying not to fall into the mining test pits. He's not the first geologist to crawl around the ridge. Over the decades, visiting professors and students have done field studies and published their findings in reports that would be downright arousing to other geologists but are an effective sleep aid to the rest of us. The ridge that the highway would cut through is a geological anomaly, created (roughly) when magma came roiling to the surface to meet an ancient underwater sea, where it pillowed into Ely Greenstone, folding itself like egg whites into a soufflé of granite and jasper and a dozen other classifications of rocks and minerals. When the seawater hit the lava and cooled it, narrow drifts of iron leached out, and *voilà*, our ridges.

From Mac we also learn that The Lake already has the highest concentration of copper sediment in the state and that the sulfide runoff from road construction could bring it even higher, as well as possibly tainting the nearby Vermilion watershed.

Because The Lake is designated a natural lake by the DNR, building codes assure that no cabin or structure can be built too close to the shore. When paddling around, one sees only a few docks; to make out cabins, you have to squint inland. Most neighbors have built modest rustic cottages. Our own is *modest*-modest, smaller than Thoreau's. I think of him with envy, banging around in his 10x15 cabin, dreaming about what I could cram into thirty extra square feet: a reading chair or a chest of drawers, a kitchen sink! And since The Lake is smaller than Walden Pond, no one much noticed it during the nineties and the era of McMansion summer homes, so only one behemoth was built here, The Lodge. The original owners had planned their dream home together, but as such projects go, each phase required more money and time than budgeted, becoming more stressful and out of control so that before floors were laid, The Lodge had become an albatross and the marriage disintegrated, a sad lesson in excessive square-foot ostentatia.

Stepping in to take the property off the couple's hands were the Legals, a partnership of lawyer and real estate developer that by definition terrifies those of us protective of our isolation, especially since the Legals already owned multiple parcels and half the shoreline. Should the highway come through to make the current private road directly accessible from highway spurs, it would be eligible for an upgrade to county road, making our parcels then legally subdividable. So far, the Legals don't appear to be planning any development, only Christian retreat weekends, a sort of "Where would Jesus camp?" camp, replete with revival tents, porta-potties, and baptisms in the weedy shallows.

Circumstances for some of us have changed. During the dozen years of their marriage, Terry and Susan had worked overtime to maintain balance, but in spite of their regard for each other, things slowly tipped and they are now separated, trying to find a new relationship that works, aiming for friendship. For now, they still share their cabin and hope to find a way for each to stay connected to the place.

Time has proven that as neighbors we all get on, liberals and Smurfs happily coexisting next to Republicans, and Christians next to atheists. It was only as we'd all gotten to know each other and settled into a community that we'd discovered the Mn/DOT plan, and now we have more than proximity in common, for everyone on The Lake will suffer if the road goes through, if not by confiscation or devaluation of lands, then at least by the noise and increased traffic. Some of us are in rather a tizzy over it while others remain calm, doing the wait-and-see thing.

I force myself to imagine leaving here, reminding myself of the four things I dislike about the place: two species of insects, one of arachnid, and the climate. I never asked myself if this latitude was best, having sort of forgotten that there are only two seasons, and both can kill you. Spring is merely an extension of winter; summers are jungly green, intense, and muggy; and autumn is entirely too brief, truncated by the long, long subarctic winters that swing in hard and fast with temps that can freeze-dry nostrils in the time it takes to cram on a knitted nose cozy. The record high is 114 degrees and the low is minus 60, a swing of 174 degrees, brutal by any standard but more so when banked against my own optimal range for well-being and sanity: a twenty-five-degree variable between 35 and 60, same as for cut flowers.

Every few years, a camera crew arrives to wring another story out of the weather, most recently for a *CBS Sunday Morning* segment called "Cold Wars," in which the correspondent exaggerates the competition between the triumvirate of towns vying for the title of "Coldest in the Nation": Embarrass, International Falls, and Tower. Tower holds the official record at -60, recorded in 1996, when Embarrass citizens got robbed after their regulation thermometer broke in mid-plummet at only -52. Readings on their unofficial thermometers went as low as -66. Most Tower citizens would concede or even root for Embarrass because everyone knows it really *is* colder there, and it wouldn't be Minnesota nice not to admit it. But to hear the folks in both Embarrass and Tower tell it, International Falls isn't even a contender and is only referred to as "Ice Box of the Nation" because it owns the legal trademark, and it doesn't hurt that they've got Rocky and Bull-winkle to back them up.

Anyone would have to wonder, why willingly choose to live in a place where simply going outside can leave a trail of fingertips? And now, during the sloggy end of August, The Lake grows a green skin and the temps hover in dog-days numbers. My inner barometer fluctuates, and I lose my desire to do or *be* much of anything, waiting for the break that must surely be coming in some thunderstorm or front roiling in from Saskatchewan.

Could I leave here? The road has begun to look unstoppable, looming like more bad weather. I've already lurched through Kübler-Ross's stages of grief: 1) *Denial*—There's no *way* these people are stupid enough to go through with this!; 2) *Anger*—Fantasizing freak accidents in which Mn/DOT project managers are tragically diced or julienned; 3) *Bargaining*—Maybe it won't be so bad? Maybe we'll get used to the noise, and Mn/DOT will compensate us with enough of a settlement to build a small cabin?; 4) *Depression*—Can no one *see* how upsetting this has all been, that I've invested blood into this place?; and finally 5) *Acceptance*—The minute pigs fly.

My crusade against the road has dragged on to the point that it takes a large file box to house all the documents, maps, letters, address lists, studies, e-mails, editorials, etc. When I open the lid little puffs of defeat waft out. Sometimes we simply allow ourselves to believe that common sense will kick in, that a state agency will have an epiphany on its own (this being the punch line). In the local paper, we've been referred to as NIMBYs, an acronym I wasn't familiar with until I read it in connection with us, and I admit, yes, *indeed, Not* In My Back Yard when it comes to wrongfully planned $22 million highway reroutes. Should we be asked for easements for wind turbines or a bike trail, I'd offer to break ground with my teeth.

Through the battle, we have highlighted the environmental impact, the inordinate amount of sulfides in the surface rock of our ridge that, if blasted or ground up to make roadbed, would cause significant runoff. Mn/DOT geologists didn't seem to find much, and rumor has it they plan to mitigate the issue. Transportation agencies in other states facing this problem have had to go back after completing such road projects and clean up sulfide messes in operations that cost several times the roads themselves. Mn/DOT responded to this information with something akin to shrugs.

We've investigated the cultural significance of the land. Plenty of anecdotal evidence indicates it was once a section of a Native trade route. The narrow line of pin oaks that crosses our property is standing evidence of Native travel, the result of acorns discarded or strewn by Dakota or Anishinaabe moving along the Birch Lake portage trail. The archaeological study that the state contracted was deemed sufficient, though it was nothing more than a random "shovel test," which entails digging no deeper than a shovel head (good luck). While we know this is an old trade route, we cannot find concrete examples on old survey maps because not all tribal records were meticulously kept.

We've pointed out that highway accident statistics don't quite match up with claims, as if they have been creatively presented to justify the reroute. The push behind the reroute was safety, yet crashes have been more prevalent on other stretches of the road. In the last two years, there have been three fatal crashes, none anywhere nearby.

Bill, the real estate broker who'd pointed me to our land, was critically injured in a crash ten miles down the road. Tragically, the young man who had caused the accident was killed instantly, and a few weeks later, on a very sad and quiet day for Ely, Bill died, too. Reading some of the many tributes and public condolences, I was not surprised to learn just how much goodwill Bill had left in his wake, accrued over decades of indiscriminately imposing habitual kindness and corny jokes on the hundreds who will miss him.

I embarked on a last-ditch effort, playing Harriet the Spy, digging around where I shouldn't, looking for some key as to why the project was moving forward against reason. I called certain individuals, posing as someone not caring much about the highway but about projects closely aligned to it and dependent on the road going through as planned. It took no great sleuthing. It was just *there*, practically lying right on the road. In about an hour, I found the connection—two projects entwined and enmeshed with political motivations fueled by the sort of good-old-boy cronyism so typical of rural enclaves. I dug some more, just to make sure I had my facts straight.

It was quite possible that my findings could throw a wrench in a long-planned, long-fraught project already years behind schedule. I was alone in my discovery, and no matter the outcome, just bringing it up would doubtless make enemies of a certain few locals. For years I'd been trying to be part of this place, but what I was about to do could easily sabotage all my efforts and backfire so that, in the end, some might take great pleasure in invoking their eminent domain.

I held on to my information for several months, and only when I was notified that heavy equipment would be dispatched to drill for mineral samples did I put my final attempt into letter form. I started and tossed several drafts. For the first time since the beginning of the battle, a letter went out with my name alone on it. I couldn't recruit any neighbors, and by this stage, half of them had grown seemingly resigned or even indifferent.

I posted the letter, and now there's really nothing to do but wait it out along with the rest of summer, with its heat index hovering around ninety most days.

It's worse in Japan, where a record heat wave has killed over a hundred people since Sam moved there. His dream of living in Tokyo has finally come true. To meet his language requirement at the U of M, he'd honed his Japanese and learned his *kanji* by flipping flash cards. He worked two jobs in order to save enough money to go, got his TEFL certificate to Teach English as a Foreign Language, and was off.

He and his girlfriend, Leah, have settled on the edge of the city in an apartment that is measured by the number of *tatami* mats it will hold—six—smaller than the cheapest room at a Motel 6. It has no air conditioning. I've seen the place via a Skype tour with Sam as guide, sweat dripping off the end of his nose like a spigot while he showed me the rusted, wobbly balcony rail that their landlord had instructed them Never To Touch. Sam admitted the reason they got the place so cheap was that the building is slated to be torn down. When the tour reached the water heater that may or may not explode, he insisted I shouldn't worry.

And I don't want him to worry about the road and the land, so I say very little. When I tell him we're going north he says, "That sounds awesome," with real longing in his voice. The place *has* gotten under his skin. Now that he's in Japan, he's come to consider the land a part of "home," and perhaps on some noisy, frenetic street corner of Shinjuku, it's occurred to him that the places like our little cabin are sometimes necessary, that time spent in nature can tuck in the frayed ends of the soul.

I occasionally tune in to NHK World TV to see what's going on in Japan. Many of the Japanese newscasters speak flawless midwestern English with no hint of accent, as if educated in Iowa. You never know what you'll find on NHK: news, cultural and travel programs, a sumo match, wildly silly talk shows, a cooking demonstration, or total weirdness, such as a game show in which contestants are given potent laxatives, and the one who holds out the longest before dashing to the door of his designated neon toilet cubicle wins a fantastic prize, like a mobile clothes-drying rack to attach to a bike or an eight-foot-high stuffed animal to occupy space in a miniscule apartment.

A few times a week, we e-mail-chat, and Sam reports adventures he and Leah are having, big and small, like going to the *Lost in Translation* bar in the Tokyo Park Hyatt and blowing their food budget for a day on one shot of Jameson and one non-alcoholic cocktail, just to see the view, just to have *been there.*

Like any mother I sometimes have to stop myself from advising, not wanting to be too much of a "smother," which Sam used to call me whenever I got on him about school or his room. He writes to say an informal version of "mother" in Japanese is *haha.*

Haha. Motherhood has been sort of a laugh in hindsight. In the beginning, I took to it not quite like a duck to water, pregnancy being quite a shock and not something I'd willingly repeat. Sam wasn't the easiest fetus, and by the time he'd finished growing elbows to work his way out with, we were both a little stunned and weary. Not one female friend or relative had warned me, making me wonder if all mothers instinctively get tight lipped about pregnancy and its grisly climax because if women really knew what they were in for, the species would doubtless screech to a halt. Men may have their secret societies and strange initiations in the basements of the Knights of Columbus, but they've got nothing on the cult of Motherhood. No hazing ritual or overweight Shriner squeezing his way out of a toy car has anything on labor and delivery.

Maybe some hormone deficiency had rendered me less maternal than most, and during that first year, not knowing how to act like other mothers, I was probably giving some wrong cues, which Sam responded to by not acting much like other babies, which was good because I hadn't really expected a *baby*, somehow. I thought I would give birth to someone to *talk* to, and while other mothers cooed and baby-talked through the milky haze of breast-feeding, Sam and I were tentative latcher and latchee. Hardly blissed out on any maternal plane, I would shake my head and ask Sam, as if he were twenty, "How weird is this?," then pick up where I'd left off reading. Sam loved "Shouts & Murmurs" in *The New Yorker*, I think because my torso so often jiggled with laughter.

He did eventually talk, and not a minute too soon. I'd been feeding him grapes, having at least enough instinct to mash them like bloated ticks so he wouldn't choke. Each time I gave him one, I repeated, "Grape." When I picked up the last one in the bowl, Sam grabbed it with an emphatic "Grape!" feeling the shape of the word in his mouth at the same time as the sweetness. A look I hadn't seen before passed over his features, as if some new gadget in his head powered up at that moment. He said it again, more thoughtfully: "Grape." He *got* it. *If I say the name of the thing, the one with breasts will give it to me!* And from then on he was able to connect a word to a person, place, or thing, and we both sighed a sigh of relief: babyhood was behind us.

When my sisters and I were kids, our mother had the famous Kahlil Gibran poem tacked to the kitchen wall so long, it eventually faded and curled.

> Your children are not your children.
> They are the sons and daughters of Life's longing for itself.
> They come through you but not from you.
> And though they are with you, yet they belong not to you.

And while I suspect my mother might have interpreted these lines as a sort of disclaimer, I read them differently, preferring the notion of parents being "the bows from which your children as living arrows are sent forth."

When people ask if I'm worried or if I miss Sam, I say, "No," and "Terribly." I'm glad he's taken this big step of moving, even if it's to live in one of the more difficult places in the world for a foreigner to acclimate to. He isn't so cool he can't ask for directions or even help, and he has a knack with people and languages. The important thing is that he's *living*, intensely. He reports they have already made several friends and taken a few trips with them, to go river rafting, to music festivals, or just *out*, which is often an adventure itself, it seems.

And as much as I miss him, I don't want him to come back anytime soon, though when he does, maybe I'll finally shake off the annoying lyrics of "I'm turning Japanese, I think I'm turning Japanese, I really think so."

⌒

I await a response to my letter to the Mn/DOT Ombudsman. As far as the heat, relief will eventually come in September. Slivered between dying summers and looming winters here are the gemlike, fleeting autumns, the ideal weeks when the bugs are dead but the leaves aren't quite, and it is *cool.* I intend to enjoy the coming months at the cabin, even if they are our last.

Twenty-one

The physical labor around the cabin never seems much like work. In his trilogy *Into Their Labours*, John Berger chronicles the lives of French peasant families who herd and tend their sheep and cows and pigs, grow their feed, milk them, process the milk into cheese, force-feed the geese, etc., wholly occupied from sunrise until dusk, only to get up and do it again with little variation day to day save the seasons changing. To hear Berger tell it, his neighbors didn't consider such endeavors as labor but as *life*, one inextricable from the other, each chore simply the next thing to be done after finishing the one before it. The future was the next harvest.

I haven't a fraction of that sort of wherewithal and no insight into what it might actually be like to live in a truly close relationship to the land, but sometimes after a long day of collecting stones or building stairs, I'm exhausted in a good way, sore, dirty, and pleased by tangible results. It's not work; it's accomplishment. And it's not done for *me*, but for this place. Maybe that's the difference between labor and a labor of love.

Things around here continue to change, sometimes slowly, sometimes less slowly. Ely was recently voted the "Coolest Small Town in America," and reactions in town are mixed. Most foresee a bump in the influx of summer visitors over the next few seasons, with a few more T-shirts and postcards being sold, but that's about it. Others worry over the prospect of more outsiders moving in, paying high prices for land and cabins, which only causes everyone's taxes to leap. This one thing, taxes, seems to be the major unifier among all cabin owners, local and not. Our common gripe.

The Ely of the present and that of my youth are forty years apart, and in between there's been nothing *but* change. Every year, the place is a little less folksy and Range-y. There are more Subarus than pickups on the streets, more Tevas than steel-toe boots, more Filson than Carhartt. These are markers of a place evolving, a place that has tapped out its resources of timber and metals and minerals and now finally shifts focus to acknowledge the surrounding wilderness to be the most valuable and sustainable thing it has going for it, the most natural resource it will ever have.

A new 2,500-acre state park is now in the works for the eastern shore of Lake Vermilion, but only by a close call, barely making it beyond gnashings over the bargaining table between state government and U.S. Steel, who planned to develop it. With Bear Head Lake State Park just down the road, some think we don't need another park and would rather have the revenue from property taxes that would result from development. But while Bear Head is the RV-friendly type of park with amenities like electric hookups and camper cabins, Lake Vermilion will be more "rustic," attracting backpackers and campers who want something nearer to a Boundary Waters experience without the hassles of permits and portaging.

Down the road, the town of Tower, which has steadily lost population since the sixties and admittedly suffers a dearth of charm, is hoping for a comeback with a master plan to revive the town with a condo-retail-restaurant-marina complex. At Dee's Lounge in Ely, Juri gives me the skinny. "Yuppie-fying the place," he says, "the whole nine yards aimed at rich 612ers."

Earl nods in agreement. "It's a lotta eggs in one basket."

They both make predictions of what they believe will be the region's fate. More local kids like their own will go off to college, get too big for their britches, and move on to bigger and better things in larger cities. Ironically, some of them will be replaced with folks who *have* bigger and better things they are willing to give up to move here.

Juri says, "And don't forget the new wave of those telecommuters—the freelance types who can live just anywhere like here and work there in cyberspace."

"And retirees. The boomers are coming." Earl holds up his wristwatch as if they're on their way. He doesn't see such trends slackening, the outcome being that in a few years, Ely "will look just like Aspen."

Those forecasts might be extreme (Aspen it isn't), but small-town populations here may well go the way Berger's French farmers did, with the youth growing up and away from rural life, leaving the old ways and the old people behind in favor of the cities and vastly different new lives. I can relate to those farmers as I can relate to Juri and Earl—we are all losing sons and daughters.

And we have lost old ways as well. Despite my heritage, I for one cannot tailor a dress, make wine or soap, knit a mitten, paint a portrait, or craft much of anything useful. But I have developed an itch to learn stone building. I'd always been charmed by the stone foundations and hearths of the old cabins and resort cottages we've stayed in, and frankly, just being around so much rock, I reason that since it's what we have the most of, why not do something with it? After wrestling stone into a crooked staircase over the course of several summers, I wanted some real instruction, and after years of threatening to take a stone-building class, I finally scraped up the tuition. Jon, sport that he is, signed on, too.

Besides, the activity would take my mind off the road. "Do something!" was Dad's mantra when he'd see me sulking, which was wildly annoying at the time but not such bad advice. True enough, the stone-building Incas probably didn't sit around fretting over how long they would get to hang out in Machu Picchu. They just got up and pushed rocks around, knowing that any minute they could get brained or maybe fall off the green edge and into the jungle below. Supposedly, for every three feet of the Great Wall built one Chinese laborer was killed (or "having tea with the ancestors"). Pious Pilgrims left their legacy of hundreds of miles of rock walls in New England. One look and you can imagine the Puritans in their goofy collars and buckle shoes, harvesting spring crops of rocks they believed were heaved up by God's frosty wrath.

Point being that in our impermanent and mortal state here on Earth, about the only thing of certainty is stone. To prepare for class, I read manuals on dry stacking along with masonry books as thrilling as their titles, learning a few intriguing terms in the process: "Cheap seducer" is a stone that appears just right for the job, but no matter how many times you pick it up and try, it doesn't cut it. "Granite kiss" is the mashing of fingertips between stones. "Boulder holder" is not what you think, but a sling allowing two or more people to lift a really heavy rock, a curious belted contraption of nylon strapping with four handles and hard to imagine in action, like Mormon underwear.

Not drawn to toil by nature, I've surprised myself by opting for such physical tasks, to pry up stone to wrangle and lug and stack and hove it and then, maybe, make something of it. I'm fit for my age but not buff, and I've never aspired to become stronger until recently, now that terms like "bone density" and "muscle mass" creep into my middle-aged vernacular. If nothing else, stonework might combat the flabby wings where my triceps used to be, what Sam used to refer to as "lunch-lady arm" and tug from behind, knowing it made me insane.

The course took place at a builders' school in the next county, about halfway between Ely and Lake Superior. Our fellow "stoners" turned out to be lovely people, which was good, since we'd be spending a week together over the course of classes. As soon as work commenced, we split into gender camps as if at a real school. We *shes* skirted around men bent on getting it done or lifting the biggest rock. And while the men worked like men, the women formed more of a collective, with continuous chatter woven around each step of our wall project, learning something of each other's lives in the process. As my father had observed, women, complex by nature (difficult), have strict criteria that must be met before committing to any relationship, no matter how casual or temporary, and men need only to both own fishing poles. We women also chose to mix our mortar by hand rather than in the grumbling cement mixer. The act was quiet and rhythmic, a bit like stirring giant batches of oatmeal. We experimented using differing measures of water, lime, and mortar until it reached a consistency perfect for mudslinging, the best way to apply mortar. When mortar is thrown, the impact dissipates air bubbles and helps it get a better suck to the stone. We took great satisfaction in applying our mortar, flinging it by the handfuls.

Drawn to the finer details of finishing work, we took pains with the final stages of our wall, polishing the faces of drying mortar with bent butter knives to make it neater and more water resistant. The men may have been able to build faster, but we could get it done *nicer.*

Our second project was more complex, everyone joining up to build a bread oven like those found in wood-fired pizza restaurants. We began by pouring a concrete base, which, after curing overnight, was topped with a skirt of boulders, then filled with gravel. Constructing a dome got interesting, with all of us offering up ideas and nine approaches to one challenge, but we got it done and took the requisite photos of us all with cement dust in our hair clustered around the finished oven.

We were instructed in only "wet" wall building with mortar and rounded rocks, when Jon and I had been hoping to learn some dry-stacking techniques for fissured and faceted rock like greenstone. Back at the land, that's what we have, an endless supply of really excellent, clean-edged, lead-heavy rock underfoot and at every turn, tumbled over every slope. If we are ever inspired to construct a fortress with parapets and ramparts, all the bits and pieces are here. If nothing else, we are rich in stone. Now that we've discovered that stone building isn't so complicated or difficult, we may be able to learn dry stacking on our own by trial and error. The basics are *very* basic, and in many ways, the endeavor is a matter of instinct and patience, and a lot like parenting in that if you can forget yourself and let the stone figure out where it best fits without forcing it, you're on the right track.

My goal is a staircase that would look as if the glacier had just happened to drop stones in a natural, serendipitous cascade. Or maybe some ancient-looking wall. Making anything look natural or effortless is always far from it, and when it is achieved, it's often not noticed (which is the point, I suppose). The most natural-looking Japanese gardens are engineered with major fuss to make them look spontaneous when indeed there is plenty of artifice, with each tree and reed and boulder placed to look as if it sprouted there but actually positioned to disguise plumbing or fixtures or to encourage drainage.

Missing Sam, I sit in the Como Park tea garden, only the merest whiff of Asia, but a geisha-sized mincing step closer to my son at least in spirit. I sit wondering, as I always do, if he's getting enough fresh air.

He and Leah have moved from the hot apartment with the deadly railing and Disney stickers on the toilet to one with air conditioning. They still share a refrigerator with another tenant and so must go to another unit when they need milk. They have a travel blog to keep us all informed and entertained, and since time-wise we are fourteen hours in their past, they call it *Hello Yesterday.* They post photos and chronicle adjusting to life as resident aliens, reporting some of the many skit-like instances they live each day, such as trying to communicate to the pharmacy clerk in halting Japanese and pantomiming the need for medication for a yeast infection. I watch for each fresh post, eager to know what they've done, had a laugh over, seen, or eaten.

↬

The highway project still prowls the edges, like hounds at bay. Rumor has it that Mn/DOT plans to mitigate the sulfide issue, and as a local insider to state agencies gently broke it to me, "If Mn/DOT does not want the DNR to find evidence of high sulfide contaminants or environmental threats, they won't." I try to follow Jon's example of Captain Practical and just calmly "wait and see," but I'm more prone to pessimism and the same stomachachy anxiety I had as a child when confronted with a math problem or an adult. The investigation I requested involving two tax-funded entities colluding to scratch each other's backs was deemed to have no solid evidence, but since the investigation took place within the agency, I expect that that was the only possible outcome, facts aside. We do not have the funds to pursue legal avenues, so another door shuts. Our next and last hope is that the DNR will hold Mn/DOT to the same rigorous environmental standards that mines must now comply with.

So now, again, we wait.

When I came here ten years ago, I had ideas for carving out a place in the woods with nostalgic, Polaroid-yellow notions of times that no longer exist, people who are gone, and a moving van full of cabin kitsch meant to invoke languid summers of the past. As Jon points out (in the kindliest manner, of course), while vintage stuff is cool, it isn't always best, citing the plaid thermos that leaks and the cowboy lamp with frayed cord that could burn the place down.

And while we've nearly succeeded in creating a home in the woods, the highway and lack of cash are simply delaying that dream. I will not say it won't happen, since as I've learned, there's no predicting the future. In the end, I *can* say (without being able to fully articulate this) that I arrived set to dwell here in a particular way but have settled on a way that might just be better. I've gotten to know this place as it is now as well as then.

Every year around Christmas, DJs on WELY read letters from local kids to Santa. Desired items have included "some disinfectant for my mom," a thirty-aught-six deer rifle, fifteen gallons of diesel, and a fan belt. This says just about everything there is to know about the character of northern St. Louis County.

We want for our kids to have everything that we did and more. In Sam's case, I wanted to somehow give him the north. All he has of his grandfather are a few stories, his war medals, and a photograph of him on a tropical airstrip wearing a bomber jacket and goggles—not quite the man Sam would have met. Dad was a little guy with a gray comb-over that stood straight up in a wind, always sucking butterscotch Life Savers. Summer and winter, he dressed in layers of conflicting plaid and quilted jacket liners, continuously hitching his pants or rattling his car keys. Dad would have dragged Sam down to the pier to feed seagulls or to collect scrap metal, taken him to haunt thrift stores, or brought him down to his basement shop, where, unlike most grandfathers, he wasn't really all that inspired and his fixes and repairs usually involved more epoxy glue than skill. He'd have taught Sam poker and cribbage and of course would have taken him fishing.

Sam asks me what sort of man his grandfather was, and I scrabble around for something he hasn't heard among the dust motes of the vault of stories I've begun to forget.

Well, there was the time he attended the funeral of a man he barely knew. After the service, Dad found himself in the receiving line at the church, dry eyed and fast approaching the family with nothing to say, unable even to remember the name of the deceased. When he couldn't rustle up any words of condolence or shuffle any more slowly, he yanked hairs out of his nose to at least come up with a few tears for the widow.

He was *that* sort of man, I tell Sam.

↬

Autumn is here, finally, with the peak of rock hunting just around the corner, when the woods are navigable, when visibility is best and stones reveal themselves against the slopes of fallen leaves. We've begun a collection of boxy greenstone for a modest beginner's project, a low retaining wall to edge the gravel patch where we pitch the screenhouse. The next pile we gather will be for an outdoor fireplace and bread oven.

Walking in the woods, I see evidence of time passing. The deer bones from an old wolf kill have gone chalky with age. The wounds of a tree struck by lightning a few years ago have now softened to gray, as its strewn limbs knit themselves sleeves of moss. On our dirt road, a glassy puddle reflects yellow aspens rattling in cerulean sky so blue it looks phony. October is definitely, positively the best time to be here.

In a dawning that has come to me with glacial slowness but with the clarity of my long-ago barefoot moment on the grassy shoreline, I've realized that while living wedged between the memories of a life and an uncertain future, perhaps the best place to be standing is here. Now.

Acknowledgments

Thanks to the Anderson Center; Cornucopia Art Center; the International Writers Programme at Hawthornden, Scotland; the Kimmel Harding Nelson Center for the Arts; the Ernest Oberholtzer Foundation; and Ragdale Foundation. All provided generous support, time, and space.

Gratitude to the residents of The Lake: Gary, for putting out that fire, and Matt, who helped fight the good fight, and Susan and Terry, steadfast friends and intrepid partners in a sometimes gnarly endeavor. The residents of Ely, Minnesota, provided much inspiration and have my respect and admiration. Earl and Juri (you know who you are)—resident diplomats, Welcome Wagon, and stand-up guys—were very helpful.

Thanks to Ann Regan of Borealis Books, who took on this book and just let me write it.

I'm grateful to my family, especially my sisters, and those sisters who came before us, The Aunts. I cannot begin to express my gratitude to Jon, for everything and then some. And then some more.

Thanks, Sam, for being exactly who you are. This land is your land.

Shelter is set in the Centaur typeface family.

Book design and typesetting by
BN Typographics West Ltd., Victoria, B.C. Canada.

Printed by Sheridan Books, Ann Arbor, Michigan.